TEAMS
That
POP

It's all about the people

BRENDAN NOLAN

 FriesenPress

One Printers Way
Altona, MB R0G 0B0
Canada

www.friesenpress.com

Copyright © 2023 by Brendan Nolan
First Edition — 2023

ISBN
978-1-03-918080-2 (Hardcover)
978-1-03-918079-6 (Paperback)
978-1-03-918081-9 (eBook)

1. BUSINESS & ECONOMICS, HUMAN RESOURCES &
PERSONNEL MANAGEMENT

Distributed to the trade by The Ingram Book Company

Table of Contents

Introduction

The objective of this book is to provide managers with an approach to the challenge of good solid team performance that is within their reach. This is an approach that evolved through twenty plus years of managing and leading multi-discipline, multi-ethnic teams.

This strategy for team management enriches the work environment by facilitating input into what individuals do and how they do it. This shift in focus towards individual development increases the level of interest and focus on the work. Productivity goes up!

The approach is applicable to many types of teams such as accounting, project management, sales, administration, and so on. In addition, improvements in performance can happen very quickly. There is no expensive project that must be completed before the benefits begin to arrive.

The book is written at a level high enough to be applicable to many situations and low enough to be practically useful for managers at all levels. It is a concise and pithy read for the busy manager.

After reading this book:

- Management mentors will have discussion points to use with mentees.

- Managers at all levels will be encouraged to try new things they may have previously contemplated.

- Newer organizations will have a different approach to management and leadership to consider.

After a successful implementation of the individual development approach to management proposed in this book, there are several big wins that will be attractive to investors, managers, and employees alike:

1. Sustainable productivity will go up.

2. The value of the organization will go up.

3. The value of individuals in the organization will go up.

4. The time devoted to more interesting and valuable aspects of the management work relative to supervision and oversight will go up.

5. Teams will be more robust and capable of adapting to change.

In maturity, the team will have two mutually supportive characteristics:

1. Leadership qualities that develop and maintain a work culture where expertise and creativity can flourish.

2. Management skills to apply tools that guide the team toward its goals through a series of objectives and in-year results.

These two characteristics do not just happen. They cannot be mandated or directed. They evolve when there is sincere interest in the team's well-being and engaging the team's interest in its work.

The implementation should not need any special investment or any especially high-performing, talented people. In my eight teams, I used the normal budget, and I accepted the people I inherited. As people moved on, the best reasonably available person for the job was chosen as the replacement. The process to maturity took about two years. The benefits were commensurate with the level of effort applied and felt almost immediately—in the positive side of: productivity, costs, absenteeism, administrative issues, quality of work, or morale in general.

The right work environment, which is critical to success, forms when the leadership and management necessary for the type of work involved is distributed throughout the team. An appropriate culture develops and provides a measure of sustainability and resilience. Over the years, I noticed that teams that work well have a feel to them. It presents itself in the work environment and such teams are a joy to be around. They pop!

Each workplace is different. There is no one correct approach, and in the details, each approach must vary. Hence, this book remains at a relatively high level to describe what must be accomplished and how that should be approached.

To succeed in this writing challenge, I structured the book in three parts.

The four sections in part one, provide an overview of my thinking on the problem, the approach to solving it, the overall solution, and implementation. After reading this part, the reader should have an appreciation of the overall intent of the strategy.

There are eleven chapters in part two, ten of which group and describe the elements of the solution. These elements are found in many if not all workplaces and should be familiar to managers. The eleventh chapter is the conclusion. This is not a prescriptive book. There will be workplaces that perhaps do not use all these elements or have additional elements or groups of elements. That is not important. What is important is that the strategy described facilitates all these management elements working together with the same overall intent as described in part one. It is not easy to get to this point, but when you get there, excellence is achieved—teams pop!

Each of the sections in part one and the chapters in part two, ends with a summary of key points. Some people may wish to read these first to assess the chapter's value to them.

Part three is comprised of three sections, one that includes all the key points from the book as an aide-mémoire, another that provides insight into how the ideas expressed in the book evolved over the years, and the last acknowledges my support team, who were vital to me to complete this writing challenge.

Preparatory Housekeeping

There are a few words that are important to the text that come into use before they are dealt with in later chapters.

Policies, Procedures, Processes, and Practices (the 4 P's). Together, policies, procedures, processes, and practices describe the formal and informal bureaucracy for an organization. They are so important to our topic that chapter 3 is devoted to them.

It is not unusual that the use of procedures and processes becomes intermingled. In this book, procedures are a series of actions conducted in a certain order or manner, while processes are a series of actions or steps toward achieving a particular end. When procedures and processes are intermingled, they may become overly complex and impede performance.

The word "practice" is used both as a noun—the customary or expected procedure or way of doing something—and a verb—the actual application or use of a plan or method as opposed to the theories relating to it.

Supervising manager. This is anyone who finds themselves managing and leading a team of people at any level in the organization, top to bottom. The critical point is that they have line responsibility for the performance of a group of people.

Team. A group of people who work together for a common purpose. A good team is more than a loose collection of individuals. A good team works to make the sum of the whole greater than its constituent parts. Teams, good and not so good, exist in all walks of life.

I hope you enjoy the read and find the content useful.

Good management, makes good managers, makes teams that pop!

Introduction: Key Points

– The objective of this book is to provide managers with an approach to solving the problem of team performance that is within their reach.

– A significant direct investment should not be required.

– The emphasis is on enriching the work environment.

– The book is not about a specific team or industry. It is written to apply to many types of teams.

– There are several big wins that are attractive to investors, managers, and employees alike.

– The solution features leadership qualities to develop and maintain a suitable work culture and management skills to guide the team toward its goals.

BOTTOM LINE: Good management, makes good managers, makes teams that pop!

Notes

PART ONE:

—

SETTING THE SCENE

I:
THE PROBLEM

Work takes energy. People start everything that happens in the workplace and are the source of that energy. The more energy people bring to the workplace, the more work can get done. Fortunately, we have moved on from forced work. Today, we use incentives to encourage people to bring as much energy as they can to work. We improve how we use that energy through all the documents that govern, direct, or otherwise control how an organization operates—the policies, processes, procedures, and practices (the 4 P's)—usually supported by software tools.

It is my experience that the accepted approach to these 4 P's can leave a lot in the tank. How do you get at and release that energy?

The idea that the manager's role is to "release the power of a team" (an idea that I first heard expressed on a management course at the The Institute, which was a Canadian federal government training facility operated by Public Works and Government Services Canada) is an interesting one. A manager who was too controlling limited the team to his or her power. A manager who was too loose lost a lot of energy through confusion. My interpretation was that the manager had to have the level of management exactly right for the team and the situation. It has been my experience that a shift in focus from pure results toward developing the team generated a better return on investment.

The challenge is how to maximize the amount of energy a team can apply to the work by making better use of the available people, resources and infrastructure rather than acquiring something or someone new.

The Problem: Key Points

– People are the source of energy in the workplace.

– The more energy the team members bring to the workplace, the more work gets done.

– We want to make it easier for people to work at their capacity, and then use that capacity wisely.

BOTTOM LINE: The problem is how to maximize the amount of energy a team can apply to the work by making better use of what is available rather than acquiring something new.

Notes

II:
THE APPROACH

My starting premise is that people want and like to work. Workplaces can make that difficult, and this situation should be avoided. We want to make it easier for people to work at their capacity, and then use that capacity wisely. This requires a work environment that allows this to happen.

Culture

Many things make up a work environment. I think the most significant of all is the work culture. It should be the thing we can adjust with minimal investment. We seek a culture where the people want to:

– Come to work.

– Contribute; put in a solid, productive shift for which they are properly rewarded.

– Go home feeling satisfied with their day.

  I focussed on three things:

– Team interactions.

– Understanding the work.

– Encouraging personal development.

  Work in the above three areas resulted in teams that:

- Worked well together and respected those with whom they interacted.

- Made excellent decisions about the work without referring to their manager.

- Grew in confidence and ability. This also resulted in a nice, gentle turnover of team members as people moved on to other bigger challenges.

- Were not administrative problems.

- Achieved the desired results, under budget and ahead of schedule.

- Were resilient. The teams adjusted and adapted quickly to change, taking it in stride, barely skipping a beat.

Attitude, Approach, and Application

All the above can only be accomplished by people who have a certain attitude toward their work. For great team performance, this *attitude* brings with it an openness to find a good *approach* to the work and the individual *application* to see the task through to completion.

Attitude

I noted the following common attitude attributes in my teams.

Work ethic. Everybody must put in a fair day's work for fair pay. In my experience, this covers a considerable part of the population. Most people need to work to some degree or another, and work should be productive and rewarding.

Sincerity. Mean what you say, and say what you mean. It is not always possible, but the intent should always be so.

Openness. It takes courage to be open. To have a team perform at a higher level, the team must trust itself.

Do what you say, say what you do. Try to lead and manage by example. Hypocrisy does nothing to aid team performance.

Approach

Every problem needs a good approach. There is always more than one way to do something, and selecting a path is a skill that develops with time and practice.

Application

Application is the capacity to commit to a work project for the duration required.

Goal, Vision, and Mission Statements

In addition to these three qualities, when it comes to getting the required results, I am a fan of simple goal, vision, and mission statements. Together with realistic objectives and a results plan, they are fundamental to getting things done and done right. Discussing and agreeing on these statements is best done over time with the team in the workplace. A retreat is sometimes necessary to achieve the final focus.

Workplaces can be complicated. We want team members to overcome or work around barriers to progress by thinking and acting accordingly. A simple goal statement serves to remind them of what the team is working toward.

I prefer:

– Goal statements that provide a directional beacon for team members.

– Vision statements that describe what the goal will look like when it is realized.

– Mission statements that describe broadly how the goal and vision will be achieved.

– Objectives that describe the route to the goal.

– Enabling objectives, if required, for the steps to achieve an objective.

– Results plans that drive the team toward the objectives. There can be more than one results plan (chapter 7).

The Approach: Key Points

– How to nurture a successful work culture is what we need to understand.

– Focus on three things:

  · Team interactions.

  · Understanding the work.

  · Encouraging personal development.

– Frame the approach through goal, vision, and mission statements. Mark the route to success with objectives and a results plan.

BOTTOM LINE: The right ATTITUDE brings with it an openness to find the right APPROACH and the individual APPLICATION to see the task through to completion.

Notes

III:
THE SOLUTION

To recap, the problem is how to maximize the amount of energy a team can apply to the work by making better use of what is available rather than acquiring something new.

Goal, Vision, Mission Statements, and Objectives

For our problem, goal, vision, mission statements, and objectives are:

Goal. Maximize the amount of energy a team can apply to the work by making better use of what is available rather than acquiring something new.

Vision statement. A work environment where challenges are accepted willingly, and individuals develop and maximize their contribution to the team's results.

Mission. To create result-focussed work environments that contain the components in figure 1. These components are loosely integrated by an information infrastructure and a balance of distributed management, leadership, and *followership* capabilities in the team.

Followership. Leadership 101 is that to lead you first must know how to follow. Good followers contribute to the overall solution. They ask questions, make suggestions, accept, and follow direction.

Objectives:

1. Develop the right supervising manager.

2. Mature the culture.

3. Focus on the work.

4. Evolve the policies, processes, procedures, and practices.

5. Create a role-based team structure.

6. Establish effective priority management.

7. Concentrate on results.

8. Build effective change management.

9. Enable requirements management.

10. Set up communications through the information structure that controls the work.

Management Model

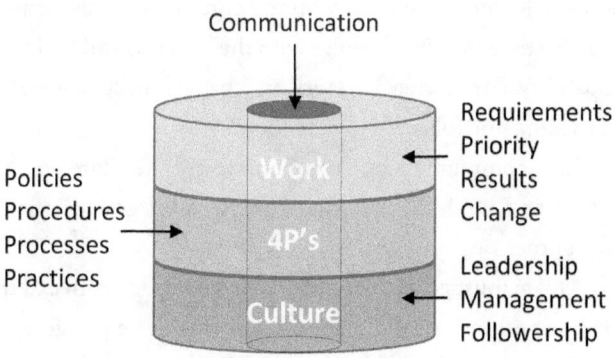

Fig 1 Management Model

Figure 1 shows the arrangement of the components of the management model that I used. Think of it as a three-layer cake, where the work part is as large as possible.

The bottom layer is the resource layer and the source of team energy. Resources can be many things. In this book, they are people and money. The combination of leadership, management, and followership create the culture. This is the primary force in releasing the resource energy for the work. There are other factors, such as facilities, tools and so on, that influence the amount of energy released. But, the critical factor, in my experience, is the culture. A person's compatibility with their work and work culture is a factor in the amount of energy released for work. Choosing the right people for the work is critical to good team performance.

The middle layer contains the policies, procedures, processes, and practices (the 4 P's). This layer applies the resource energy to the work. For good team performance, the 4 P's must suit the team and the work.

The top layer represents work. Requirements, priorities, and results focus the energy on the core work. Teams cannot remain static they must evolve with the business and their own capability. For this reason, work on "change" must be included in a team's portfolio.

The communication component is the core of the model and binds all parts together. It is integrated into the work processes.

A team must get results and sustain an impact from external change with minimal disruption. For this to be possible, the cake must have the right properties. For example, in addition to the 4 P's suiting the team, the balance in management, leadership, and followership is not the same for all organizations.

The properties depend on the preparation, mix, and integration of the model's parts.

Because it is such a complex, almost organic process, it is better to let things evolve. It is the supervising manager's job to keep things moving in the right direction.

The parts generally develop in parallel and at a different pace, not sequentially. The gaps close as the team approaches its mature end state. For each of my six teams, this took one to two years. But, because of the continuous improvement process, benefits were quickly visible.

Finally, while it is better if all teams in larger organizations share the same approach to their work, it is not necessary. A single unit can work this way. The supervising manager needs reasonable autonomy in the work area, and the organizational interfaces must be manageable for the team.

Fortunately, it was my experience, that team members schooled in this approach to working, improved their ability to manage organizational interfaces.

– Team members were better prepared to work at these interfaces.

– The information model (chapter 10) made it easier to pass accurate information when needed.

– They knew which information they needed for their work and that which was generated for, or received from others.

The Solution: Key Points

– The management model is a three-layer cake comprised of twelve components.

– For any team, the parts to this cake will have a different preparation, mix, and integration to achieve a well-performing team that is resilient in change.

– A person's compatibility with their work and work culture is a factor in the amount of energy released for work.

– Choosing the right people for the work is critical to good team performance.

– Develop the model through the parallel pursuit of ten objectives.

BOTTOM LINE: The model evolves through a complex, almost organic process. The components generally develop in parallel and at a different pace, not sequentially.

Notes

IV:
IMPLEMENTATION

Like the management model, the ten objectives in part one, section III do not progress sequentially. There is a start order, but once started, the objectives progress in parallel. Eventually, when the objectives are met and the components of the management model are formed, the team approaches its sustainable performance level as the vision is realized. Remember your vision statement: *A work environment where challenges are accepted willingly, and individuals develop and maximize their contribution to the team's results.*

The implementation start order is:

Step 1. Find the person who will be the supervising manager to guide the management model and be the kernel about which the culture forms (chapter 1).

Step 2. Start the formation of the foundational layer of the management model. Begin establishing the culture (chapter 2) by using the 4 P's (chapter 3), the work (chapter 4), and role-based team structures (chapter 5) as the discussion vehicle.

Step 3. Start the middle layers of the management model by picking one or more local processes that are not satisfactory or work planning (chapter 6), results management (chapter 7), requirements management (chapter 8), change management (chapter 9), or communications (chapter 10). A team will be strong in one area. Start with that, and the other areas will get pulled along with it.

Step 4. Continue working on all aspects of the culture and continuously seek improvements to the model and end products using requirements and change management.

The working model (figure 1) is complicated. It is challenging and perhaps impossible to get everything "just so." Improvement can only happen if there is a sustained commitment. Performance targets need to be challenging and within reach without exhausting everyone. It was my experience that teams have strength in one area that they tend to favour. Allow this area to develop. The team will see that it can only progress so far before it must work on its weaknesses. The strong area will pull the rest with it. Focus on what is critical to achieving results, and do the easiest first!

I also observed that team members had two toolsets: a personal toolset of character qualities (ref. part 2, chapter 2, "Establish the Culture") and a non-personal one related to their area of work, such as accounting, project management, analyst skills and knowledge, and so on. When my teams were working well, the personal and non-personal toolsets worked well together individually and across the team. The better these tools are applied, the better the distributed level of leadership, followership, and management across the team, the better the results, and the better the team's resilience in change. The team adapts and moves on.

To be sure a team is at its maximum capacity, seek to improve through small changes to processes, procedures, or practices, and then observe the results. Performance may or may not improve. A continuous improvement approach means that the operation is always being examined with a critical eye, seeking opportunities to improve. Small changes are less risky, and if an error occurs, it is usually not a big issue to go back.

Implementation: Key Points

- There are four steps: pick the leader, start the culture, develop the model, and continuously improve.

- Results objectives should be challenging but not exhausting.

- To ensure the team remains at its best, continue to seek improvements through small changes that can be reversed if required.

BOTTOM LINE: A culture appropriate to the workplace that is guided by an effective, efficient, and economic management model will, in a continuous improvement activity, generate the right environment and get results.

Notes

PART TWO:

THE ROUTE TO THE SOLUTION

Chapter 1

THE SUPERVISING MANAGER

Generally speaking, management and leadership are open to a large part of the population, and everyone has to start somewhere.

Managers come in many forms. Financial managers, account managers, factory managers, and building managers, to name a few. A supervising manager is any manager who manages a team and this, for me, implies some leadership component. For the purposes of this book, supervising a team is a significant aspect of their work.

This chapter talks about the role of supervising managers and some things they should keep in mind when approaching this initiative, understanding the work, and building team relationships.

Supervising managers are crucial to attaining the goal in the manner intended by the vision and mission statements. They require the positive core behaviours, described in chapter 2, that are suitable for their role in building the right environment, where they set and maintain the standard for the culture and oversee the development of the management model. The right attitude and a commitment to the culture is required, while the requirement for prior

Vision statement. A work environment where challenges are accepted willingly, and individuals develop and maximize their contribution to the team's results.

knowledge and experience related to the subject depends on the situation and expectations. Generally, the higher and more pressing the expectations, the deeper the knowledge and experience requirement.

Role

Supervising managers provide the core for the culture, and they use the following skills to nurture the team as it builds the management model.

Oversee the work and the evolution of the team. This is to ensure it progresses in the right direction. Workplaces usually have issues. The supervising manager's job is to make sure these issues are dealt with before they become distractions. Judging when and how to insert yourself into an issue and guide it to resolution is a skill. Like all skills, it develops with time and practice. Understanding the work and the people is crucial to guiding the supervising manager's need and timing to act. In *In Search of Excellence*, Tom Peters and Robert H. Waterman Jr. talk about experience referring to H.D. Simon's thoughts

Mission. To create results-focussed work environments that contain the components in figure 1. These components are loosely integrated by an information infrastructure and a balance of distributed management, leadership, and followership capabilities in the team.

When I first started in management—over forty years ago—I had a boss who believed that intelligence could compensate for lack of experience by as much as 80 percent. While this is broadly true, he did not say that the precious piece is the other 20 percent. Everybody who wants to manage, and lead, must start somewhere. You only gain valuable experience by doing your best, examining the failures, learning from them, and then moving on to the next. In this way your "vocabulary" develops.

on chess masters and management thinking. As chess masters recognize patterns and build a vocabulary of these patterns, so do managers by building similar professional vocabularies through their training and work experiences. We experience this in action when a younger, less experienced manager sees that the more experienced manager just seems to know the answer. It is almost intuitive! The idea of a developed vocabulary of patterns explains it. The more experienced manager knows when something does not sound or feel right. They know enough to know that something is missing.

Encourage thinking and initiation based on solid reasoning. When a team member asks a question, this is an opportunity to discuss a topic. Lead or guide the team member through a discussion to arrive at the answer themselves.

Keep the "good-idea fairies" in check. Most people have "good ideas" that are not so good on another day. This is a good-idea fairy.

The nature of ideas is that a fair number are either obviously non-starters or, worse, not so obviously non-starters. The supervising manager should recognize the latter and walk the team through the thinking process to illustrate why the idea is not as good as one might think. It is not a question of letting an originator down slowly. It is about illustrating that waste is very much part of the good-idea business. You want team members to come forward with their ideas because the really good idea remains silent if they do not.

Ensure the team does not wander off course and lose sight of its goal. This is like keeping the good-idea fairies in check, except this is more about navigating through a situation or problem. It is easy to take a wrong turn and end up at a dead-end. The supervising manager's job is to keep their or the team's head up to be aware of an approaching and potentially wrong turn, and then steer the team to the right choice.

Identify, adapt, and use situations to improve upon weaknesses (your own and others). Weaknesses in the team do not necessarily reveal themselves directly. They might present themselves as symptoms, such as frequent mistakes or other adverse situations. Instead of reacting to a symptom, take stock of other negatives. Is there a common cause? Discuss it, and then explain how it negatively impacts the work or their work environment. It is best to address the cause in a work context so the team can feel the improvement.

It is not an infrequent occurrence that mistakes occur because a person or persons do not understand their job and why they are doing it. A discussion on their work and its value will result in improved performance almost overnight. It also does happen, in a team new to you, that during this discussion you find you don't understand why the person is doing what they do either! Work through it together. The result is always better for everyone.

If weaknesses are not evident, the team is working within its potential. If the wheels are not threatening to come off somewhere, the team is not working close to its potential. You might ask yourself the question: Is the team sufficiently challenged?

Appropriate challenges support team development and personal growth. They should be fun things to do; look for suitable ones. Teams that are not appropriately challenged become bored and lose focus, and performance will drop off.

Integrate weaknesses with strengths to generate the whole. Nothing in a team happens in isolation, and no two people have the same set of strengths and weaknesses. There is no barrier between stronger areas and weaker ones. The supervising manager's job is to mix and match the work assignments and people to cover off weaknesses and provide the opportunity to develop strength.

Be fair and even handed. In today's interconnected and mobile world, supervising managers need to be more aware and sensitive to cultural differences. (If you have not appreciated it yet: how you treat your people is fundamental to good team performance!) Our work teams today are more of an eclectic mix than they were twenty or even ten years ago. Incorporating these differences into the workspace contributes to the team building process, facilitating fairness and even-handed treatment of team members. People in this environment will work to cover for their teammates for a short while. The work still must get done; it is, after all, work, and not recreation.

In our target work environment, results should be without bias or prejudice. If a request could be met without unduly and negatively impacting the results program, there is no reason not to grant it. Similarly, if the results program is materially impacted that would be sufficient reason not to grant a request.

> I granted many more requests than I refused. The team always covered off and found a work around. That's the teamwork that I am talking about!

Recruit the best available people for the work. If you do not understand the work, then choosing the best of the available people for a particular job is a matter of chance. If results are a priority, then choosing the right person for the job is not about friendship, or choosing someone you like, or someone of the same cultural background. Seek and choose the people who have the necessary background for the job, and who will give you what they think and not what you think.

Supervising managers keep their heads up to look over, around, and into the team. They stay in touch with progress and events in the group and at its interfaces with other organizations. The work and the team must head in the right direction.

If all this seems a bit daunting, do not be alarmed. It takes time to build vocabulary patterns. But if you do not try to do the work, then that vocabulary will never develop. If you keep at it, you will improve. Attitude, approach, and application are absolutely vital!

The Approach to the Environment

The work environment we seek cannot be directed or ordered. Instead, it is nurtured by building relationships and encouraging supportive attitudes from day one, through a focus on work and effective communications.

Initially, supervising managers seek information from team members. Early on, the exchange of information is a dialogue of honestly held opinions, views, and assessments of situations. An active exchange develops a better understanding of the subject. By "active," I mean that the participants are focussed on the discussion to understand the message. The dialogue demonstrates understanding. A sentence makes sense relative to what has gone before it. They are not just focussed on making sure their body language suggests they are engaged!

The team knows that they should tell you what they think. In a discussion, it is OK to have a different point of view. The sharing of viewpoints provides mentoring and learning opportunities and a more detailed and common understanding of the problem. A better solution always results.

There will be times when decisions appear to lack consistency with the inputs provided by the team. In our target environment, it is OK to ask and answer respectful questions about such decisions. Once the question is asked and answered, it should not come back again. The workplace is not a democracy. While consensus agreement is preferred, it is not essential for progress. Little, if any, of the above will happen straight away. It takes time and patience.

Beginning Transformation

Releasing a team's power is about building on something that exists, is stable, and running reasonably well. It is not in a downward spiral. When confronted with an organization in crisis, a more autocratic style is required. Relationships remain essential to finding the correct cause of the issue and resolving it quickly. These circumstances often need tough decisions; feelings will likely get bruised. Active communication needs to demonstrate consistency in decisions and the absence of favouritism. Once team survivability is assured, the work on the transformation can begin.

Look to action changes that improve on the "as-is." Small changes to current practices—the customary or expected procedure or way of doing something—are low-risk activities. If they do not improve performance, they can be reversed.

Seek and find the answers to these questions about the work: what? why? who? when? where? how? This applies to everybody on the team and the work they do.

Resist the temptation to make your mark. There is usually a good reason why things are the way they are. Find out what that is before starting work on your contribution to the team.

"Hit the ground running" are the words I least like to hear. I much rather people hit the ground and stand still to see which way the team is going and then work to influence that direction.

At all times, keep the goal front and centre in your mind. Maximize the amount of energy a team can apply to the work by making better use of what is available rather than acquiring something new, such as new software, a new tool, a new team member, a new building, and so on.

Understand the work. Take the time to understand why things are the way they are. It is essential to know if the reasons are still valid. It may take days, weeks, or months, depending on the size and complexity of the operation; however, a complete understanding is not required to advance. When making an adjustment, there needs to be reasonable assurance that a wheel will not come off the wagon. If it does, then have a plan ready to put it back on again. If you do not do this, then you will never develop the experience vocabulary.

Build a relationship with team members. Team members need an opportunity—scheduled or impromptu—to express their views without fear of reprisal. Issues that are bubbling below the surface will often come up in discussion. Engage team members in conversations to explore and comprehend what they might be. In a one-on-one setting, a supervising manager can focus on the individual. Such meetings provide all team members with an opportunity to express themselves outside of a team setting.

Deal with issues. Frequently, an issue is not as expressed. A short discussion, some additional information, or a short explanation can clear it up in little or no time. Sometimes, more work is required to come to grips with the situation: research to gather more information, discussions with other involved people, and so on. It is not necessarily the supervising manager's job to do all the work. It is better if the person with the issue does as much of the work as possible. Keeping the workplace free of issues, or as free as can be expected, is the supervising manager's job.

Issues must be dealt with. They are either resolved with a solution or accepted and accommodated as a fact of life. Progress or changes in circumstances can evolve a fact of life into a problem with a solution. It does not hurt to revisit old issues to see if a solution now exists. Our recent lives are replete with big examples of this phenomenon. Think, for a moment, how our lives would have been during the COVID-19 pandemic without the Internet! No Amazon and perhaps no efficient and effective contactless delivery service at all! Remote working without broadband communication systems would be impractical. People would have had to risk normal work procedures, or their companies would have gone under. In the workplace, the examples are there, just not so large and apparent as these ones.

Do not allow revisiting old issues to facilitate foot-dragging. Deal with the issue and move on. There are people who like to keep issues going. Rewording the same question to see if they can get a different response is a common tactic. The supervising manager does not tolerate this behaviour.

Lastly, team members must accept that supervising managers are loyal to the chain of command. Sometimes, a discussion cannot be as open as one might like. The supervising managers' primary work loyalty is to the organization.

The Supervising Manager: Key Points

- Supervising managers provide the core for the culture.

- During the process they:

  - Oversee the evolution of the team.

  - Encourage thinking and initiative.

  - Keep the "good-idea fairies" in check.

  - Ensure the team does not wander off course and lose sight of its goal.

  - Identify and use situations to address weaknesses.

  - Integrate weakness and strength to generate a whole.

  - Are fair and even handed.

  - Recruit the best available people for the work.

- Supervising managers keep their heads up to look over, around, and into the team to keep it safe and on track.

- Relationship building and supporting attitudes are columns around which the team can form.

- Releasing the power of the team is about building on something that is stable and functioning.

- Resist the temptation to make your mark.

- Understand the work before beginning the transformation.

- Encourage the expression of honestly held views.

- Resolve issues or accept them as facts of life that one must work with.

BOTTOM LINE: The supervising manager sets the tone for the team from day one. They provide the leadership for the evolving culture and supervision for the developing management model.

Notes

Chapter 2
ESTABLISH THE CULTURE

Good team performance is the outcome of the work culture we seek. While team members and supervising managers have different roles in creating this culture, they share a commitment to certain behaviours and skills described in this chapter.

Target Culture

Our target culture must encourage understanding of the work and be permissive in allowing team members to perform at their capability level.

After selecting the supervising manager, work on the culture can start on day one on the job.

Team culture is a foundational element of solid team performance. It is my experience that people who understand the work perform better. The deeper the understanding, the better the performance. A deeper understanding comes with the doing of the work.

Revisiting the Goal, Vision, and Mission Statements

Goal. Maximize the energy a team can apply to the work by making better use of what is available rather than acquiring something new.

Vision statement. A work environment where challenges are accepted willingly, and individuals develop and maximize their contribution to the team's results.

Mission. To create results-focussed work environments that contain the components in figure 1. These components are loosely integrated by an information infrastructure and a balance of distributed management, leadership, and followership capabilities in the team.

The Management Model

We wish our target culture to encourage people to give their energy in the workplace, which we then accept and use wisely. The culture is generated by the people, but the management model is the structure or framework to maintain focus on the work. A better management model encourages people to give their energy, is open to receiving it, and is better at using it.

Figure 1 presents a three-layer management model that we seek to implement. It was described in some detail in part one section III, "The Solution." The energy in a team exists in the bottom layer of the model. It is applied to the work (the top layer) through the 4 P's in the middle layer.

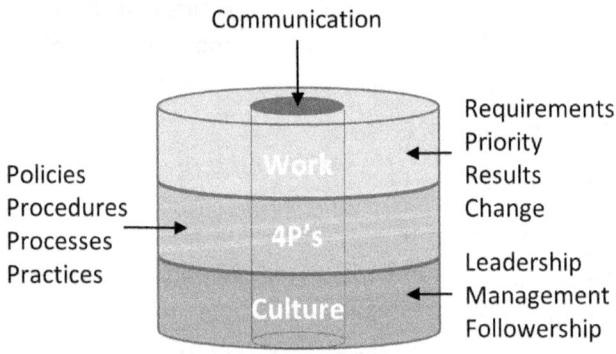

Communication

Requirements
Priority
Results
Change

Leadership
Management
Followership

Policies
Procedures
Processes
Practices

Work
4P's
Culture

Fig 1 Management Model

The 4 P's may deter or resist team members putting their available energy into the work. They also may not be efficient in using that energy. We aim to construct a set of 4 P's that:

– Do not act as a barrier to people putting their energy into their work.

– Use that energy wisely.

In the overall management model, for good team performance the 4 P's must suit both the team and the work and vice-versa. Team participation in the development of the 4 P's is vital. The better the team understands their work, the more valuable is their participation. This leads to a better management model more suited to the team, the work, and an improved team performance. This activity, in turn, improves the understanding of the work. The process is circular. It continues until the team arrives at its potential. Then, it flattens out to accommodate the changes endemic to any business.

Positive Core Behaviours

Developing the culture can start on day one through discussions about the work and the 4 P's. The quality of the leadership is crucial to the success of these discussions. Good leadership will encourage good followership and the sought-after core behaviours as mentioned below.

Throughout my working life, the subject of leadership versus management has surfaced from time to time. I found it useful to consider management, leadership, and followership as commodities. The better the distribution of these three commodities, the more robust the team. It was better able to accept and adapt to change and more successful at identifying and resolving issues.

Because people grow under these conditions, they will move to new opportunities. Expect a turnover of personnel that adds new ideas and experiences. This is a positive. It is healthy for the team to have a gentle, non-disruptive flow of new people arriving, bringing fresh ideas and challenging old ones.

The following behaviours are encouraged.

Openness. In pursuit of the target environment, being open is a quality that the supervising manager must bring to the team. It is the first foundation stone. Try to be receptive and responsive to all questions in a way that addresses every issue.

Straightforwardness. Supervising managers build trust with the team by being straightforward. They are straight shooters and call it as they see it, dealing with issues before the team's attention from the desired results is diverted.

Understanding. People's private and work lives do not happen independently of each other. Occasionally they clash. When this happens, nearly everyone needs a favour or consideration when the terms of employment do not cover the situation. From time to time, such a thing also happens for the organization. Favours and consideration cannot be a one-way street. There must be a fair "give and take."

- Know what is acceptable in the parent organization and avoid setting an unwanted precedent.

- Ensure the team will not be unduly burdened by the granting of a favour or special consideration.

- Avoid creating a permanent expectation that such favours will be granted.

- Consistency in decisions is important.

Flexibility. A problem has more than one solution. Teams that participate in the solution tend to want to take ownership of it. It is better if supervising managers use their expertise to guide the team and facilitate the solution. This may not be possible at first, but it should come as the culture matures.

There are two advantages to this:

1. The understanding of the work develops more quickly. This improves the energy released and how it is used for the work.

2. The supervision task is reduced, freeing up a supervising manager's time to look at longer-term issues.

Relationship building. People create the work environment. Take time to know the team members. Knowledge of situations that might impact the workplace can be a good thing, especially if that makes it possible to relieve distress.

Respectfulness. People that respect each other will respond in a manner that is consistent with a shared conversation. Being fair and direct with people or being a "straight shooter" is critical to this form of respect.

Competence. Competent people are generally more open. They are better able to generate respect, support relationships, and be straight with others.

Competence is critical to the culture. It is assessed at the team and individual level. Team members that have low levels of competence in a

Competence: the quality or extent of having the necessary ability to do something. The word "incompetent" is seldom helpful. A more helpful way is to assess the level of competence in a subject required for a particular job. People have a sufficient or lower level of competence for the work. I recommend leaving the term "incompetent" for the rhetoric of politicians.

particular aspect of the work are supported by the other team members while their competence develops.

Positive Enhancing Factors

Decision-making/taking ability. It does not take much for simple decisions to get complicated. Recognizing these situations and dealing with them correctly is a skill that takes time to develop. If in doubt, take it one step at a time. For performance, progress is important. There is nothing so demoralizing as standing still for too long.

Good decisions require the right knowledge of the topic. Experience provides a reservoir of knowledge, and people have different abilities to interpret and apply their knowledge. For this reason, different people have dissimilar additional information demands for the same decision.

There comes a time when a person can sense whether a decision is a good one or a poor one. This does not happen overnight. It grows on you through your experiences, not only in life but also in work. It's that valuable 20 percent of experience, or Simon's vocabulary (chapter 1), at work.

Communication skills. In the time before personal computing devices hit the planet, the problem was often one of incomplete, sparse information, with holes in it. Today, networks, Inter- or Intranet, are flooded with information, and that makes finding trustable information a task—sometimes an onerous one. The good news is we are getting better at this information aspect of the task.

In the aspect of successful individual communication, there is always three parts: sending, receiving, and verifying correct understanding. This may be through an active and engaged dialogue or by observing a post-communication behaviour. For example, if someone asks you for directions and you tell them to turn left, do they subsequently make a left, a right, or any turn at all?

Proper use of common communication tools. Email, presentations, written documents, and meetings are core communication tools. It is relatively straightforward to turn them into non-communicating tools.

– Email. To know that addressees have read and understood an email, ensure you receive an engaged response.

– Presentations. Get the point across in six slides. Any more than that and the message starts to degrade.

– Briefings that are lengthy are always problematic.

  · Try to bring the important points to the front without destroying the flow.

  · Know your audience and tailor the brief accordingly. One size seldom fits all.

  · After you have prepared the brief, review it to take out any material that can support the question-and-answer period. Hold it in reserve for use during that period, as required.

– Writing. Develop the argument in two pages or less—a skill that needs a lot of practice, months, perhaps years.

  · The weighty tome is challenging to read.

  · The other extreme of being overly brief provides nothing actionable.

  · The content must be concise and on topic.

– Meetings. A meeting that lasts longer than an hour usually loses some of its worth. The best meetings have:

  · A reasonable agenda.

  · A strong chairperson who can manage discussions and keep them moving.

  · Discussions that are on topic, brief, and to the point. Not always easy or possible.

Knowledge, experience, attitude, and intelligence. In the workplace, these four factors tend to come together as one when getting a job done. To a degree, they can compensate for each other. Of the four, knowledge and experience are the easiest for most supervising managers to improve upon. Intelligence can compensate for a lack of knowledge or experience, but only so far. The right attitude is fundamental to the culture needed to generate and sustain the environment. It is the hardest thing to change.

The Role of the Supervising Manager

Supervising managers set the example for behaviour and assign and monitor individual development work. The assignment of development work can be tricky. The gap between the knowledge and skill levels required for a particular job and what the available people possess can be quite large. Yet, the work still must get done! Some people thrive on this kind of challenge, while others need more support to get comfortable with the task.

The supervising manager finds the means to provide the support to get the work done. A combination of coaching, mentoring, on-the-job training, and a formal course usually suffice. Formal courses are more valuable when the team member has had some time in their job. They can relate more to what the instructor has to say and get more from the course.

The Role of Team Members

While doing the work, team members adapt their work interactions to be consistent with the target culture. They need to know the following is expected of them in the target culture:

— Actively support the behaviours listed at the start of this chapter.

— Actively participate in the development of the management model.

Team members need to be curious about the work. Understanding the answers to the questions what, who, when, where, why, and how is the target. They also need to be respectfully and ruthlessly critical of the management infrastructure. Question it, then work to improve it. This is great followership and vital to making the team pop!

Vital to their thinking skills is discussing:

— The intention and interpretation of work rules to appreciate:

   · When they can be hard, firm, or soft.

   · When and under what circumstances some rules can be broken or bent.

   · What rules are held inviolate!

— Team roles and boundaries.

— Rules that have unintended adverse effects.

Implementation Considerations

The leadership, followership, and management abilities of team personnel. The target culture cannot be forced. It evolves with the team chemistry and seldom at a speed that most people like. Time and patience are required. Management, leadership, and followership interact in the team to affect how the chemistry builds.

Across a team, there is a mixed bag of these three qualities. In some team members, they occur naturally. Others in the group work to develop them. And, for some, they somehow simply happen. Team members develop skills at a speed that depends on the individual, the team, and the supervising manager's expertise.

The type and strength of pressure under which the team is working impacts both the individual and the overall process. I found that a team responding to a clear and definite imperative type of task improved more quickly than when the importance of a job was less clear.

Relationships. The cultural transition starts with the relationships that form in the workplace. Knowledge of someone's background and their skill sets is always helpful.

Open discussion is an excellent way for team members to understand each other and build respect. Personal stories applicable to the topic can add interest to the subject and explain a point. There is no shortage of workplace topics—for example, processes, procedures, policies, rules, dos and don'ts, priorities, organizational structure, roles, job descriptions, and the need for and nature of performance evaluation.

Attitudes. Individual attitudes are important. Team members should come to work:

– To get things done.

– Ready to engage.

– Prepared to take direction or lead as required.

There are always people with a less-than-ideal attitude and who are a good deal less cooperative than others. Such people present a personal leadership event. Work with them to adjust their attitude but not at the team's expense. If the person is not capable of doing the work, that is a different problem that usually requires a different solution. Otherwise, be firm and fair. Identify and work with their strengths while helping with their weaknesses; however, keep in mind that management/ leadership is not a popularity contest. It is about getting the job done and getting it done right, on time, and under budget.

Management model. Management infrastructure comprises the policies, procedures, processes, practices, and choice of tools. For good performance, this model must meet the team's requirements.

A new team can change quite rapidly. Management structures should not be too tightly integrated or overly prescriptive. A more mature team evolves slowly and the work environment should be more stable.

For good team performance in either case, it is crucial to continuously ensure that the model remains aligned with the team's needs. This is easier with a thinking-empowered team that is aware of its environment and accepts individual responsibility.

Now the management model must be implemented, and the work continued, while the culture evolves!

Establishing the Culture: Key Points

- People are the source of team energy. Culture determines how much of that energy is released for work.

- A better management model encourages people to give their energy, is open to receiving it, and is better at using it.

- Commitment to certain behaviour patterns is a make-or-break item.

- Management, leadership, and followership are not separate entities. They are commodities distributed throughout the team.

- There are several positive core behaviours: openness, straightforwardness, understanding, flexibility, relationship building, respectfulness, and competence.

- There are several positive enhancing factors: decision making/taking ability, communication skills, knowledge, experience, attitude, and intelligence.

- Supervising managers set the behaviour example and assign and monitor individual development work.

- Team members actively support the list of behaviours.

- Team members are curious about their work. They are active in the development of the management infrastructure. Question it, then work to improve it.

- The target culture cannot be forced. Team chemistry must form naturally and that requires time and patience.

- Relationships in the team are fundamental to success.

- Team members should come to work:

- · To get things done.

- · Prepared to engage.

- · Prepared to take direction or lead as required.

– Management and leadership are not popularity contests. It is about getting the job done and doing it right, on time, and under budget.

– Management structures should not be too tightly integrated or overly prescriptive.

– A thinking-empowered team that is aware of its environment and accepts individual responsibility is essential to generating and sustaining the target culture.

BOTTOM LINE: Developing management, leadership, and followership abilities throughout the team generates a robust team that will get results.

Notes

Chapter 3

POLICIES, PROCESSES, PROCEDURES, AND PRACTICES (4 P'S)

I suspect that paperwork is the first thing that comes to mind when people think of this topic. The unfortunate truth is that useful work needs paperwork, whether in its historical paper or more contemporary electronic forms. The problem with paperwork arises in the details. It can become a burden.

This chapter is not intended to deal with the huge volume of material available

> I recall in 2018 one of my team members said—somewhat tongue in cheek—to my new boss during her in-briefing, "We don't let the process get in the way of the work around here." What he meant (I hope) was that we kept the purpose of the process in perspective and our focus on the work.

on these four areas. It is about their role in building the culture and delivering the work.

Every organization needs some bureaucracy—not too much, and not too little. Just enough to keep it safe, effective, and efficient is the target. Together these types of work documents should support the culture and guide the team in the work to be done and done safely.

Most people like to work in teams, and many want to help the team perform better. By developing a team's understanding of the work to participate in the 4 P's formulation, the product will be better. It will be leaner and more tightly focussed on what is required to do the job. The team is more likely to follow them because they are their products. It is good if a team takes ownership, because

It is my experience, if people understand the benefit of what they are being asked to do, they generally will do it better.

when there is a sense of ownership, they want it to work.

When complete, this subject area is the heart of the management model.

It is an excellent place to:

– Start developing an understanding of the work.

– Set the tone for the group culture.

– Look at how the work is done from different angles.

– Encourage creativity.

There is always more than one way to do something. Most people are capable of creative thought, and this is an area where people should feel OK with creative discussion techniques such as brainstorming. For this reason, team members need to be comfortable in a team conversation setting.

Thinking outside the box is a popular buzz phrase. It should be encouraged once the person has learned to think inside and adjacent to their box!

This is a particular reason why the core behaviours referred to in chapter two are important.

Workable creative thinking does not happen on demand. It takes time. When a creative idea reveals itself, be prepared to accept it when it happens! *But,* be on the lookout for those good-idea fairies.

When making changes or adjustments to the 4 P's, consider the impact these will have on the organizations with which you share inputs and outputs (chapter 4). Discuss any impact before making the change. It may become clear that the change should not be made, or perhaps there is a better solution.

Where to Start, and How to Proceed?

Where to start and how to proceed? These are very good questions. The answer is not fixed. Here are some things that I found useful.

Early return. Look for the area in the team where change will have the best balance between a noticeable return and the time and the effort to realize it.

Resist the urge to formulate policy. Unless this is a brand-new team, in which case provide some direction. The policy should identify the firm dos and don'ts: generally speaking, the fewer of these the better.

Start with practices. They are the least formal and most straightforward to change for an existing team. Successful practices will guide the development of suitable procedure, processes, and lastly, policy. Remember to use the goal, vision, and mission statements and objectives to stay on the path!

Planning process. Establish objectives or enabling objectives that can be used as rest stops when they are achieved. A pause is often necessary to consolidate and harvest the improvements made to practices, processes, procedures, and policies through use. Use is the most valuable feedback option: it is real! If adjustments to completed work or planned work are required, now is the time to do this.

The evaluation period of use must be substantial. It might take a month or two to get valuable feedback based on the change's impact on the team's performance targets, and not on a knee-jerk reaction.

If a change causes a disaster, do not continue with it. Every change needs a back-out plan, which is prepared prior to making the change. This plan should describe the criteria for triggering it.

Some Consideration on Process

Processes should be straightforward and easy to follow, without constant reference to a process diagram. It should be reasonably free of decision logic and reasonably the same for large and small, routine and emergency jobs. If a shortcut exists for one job, then the work the shortcut avoids is likely unnecessary for all jobs.

The change process described in chapter 9 is an example of such a process. It is free of decision logic and applies to all changes, big and small, routine or emergency.

Each step in the process should state the conditions for it to be considered complete. These conditions should note what is required for completion, and not necessarily how it is done. Where the how is important, reference a procedure.

Should processes be tightly or loosely integrated? Teams should be as flexible as possible. Unnecessary tightness in process integration reduces flexibility.

Policies, Processes, Procedures, and Practices: Key Points

–   The 4 P's:

    ·   Are essential. Keep them to the minimum.

    ·   Guide the work and should not get in its way.

    ·   Are the heart of the management model.

–   If people understand the benefit of what they are being asked to do, they generally will do it better.

–   Understanding the work will lead to leaner, more tightly focussed guiding documents.

–   Discussing these documents will generate a better understanding.

–   Teams need to take ownership.

–   Avoid embedding decision logic in process.

–   Keep integration as loose as possible to retain flexibility.

BOTTOM LINE: Team participation in the development of the 4 P's improves the understanding of the work, which leads to a better end product in this area.

Notes

Chapter 4
THE WORK

There can be many distractions in the workplace, some of which appear related to the work. Continuous improvement activities, such as the ones proposed by this book, could be or perhaps are such an example. Such things must be executed as an integral part of doing the work and not a separate project. If it is not improving the work, then why are you doing it? It is critical to focus on and not lose sight of the core work of the organization. When in doubt, ask yourself the question: What is our work?

In this chapter, we talk a little about what impacts the work that can get done, various ways to look at the work, and what the supervising manager must do.

> I have noticed that teams focussed on their work are not so susceptible to workplace distractions.

The first thing the supervising manager must do is engage their team. Take advantage of the 4 P's. These should cover the core work of the team and if they do not, you have just uncovered one problem area. Discussions and work in this area make them good candidates for developing relationships and building leadership, management, and followership skills.

The work is an excellent way to start the culture and the management model. This begins on day one on the job with team engagement.

The Management Model

Figures 2.1 and 2.2 below show an alternate representation of figure 1 in which the white circles represent what is left in the tank referred to in chapter 1.

These white circles arise from disconnects created by the unsuitability of the quality/quantity mix of available resources to the selected work items from the priorities and unsuitability of the 4 P's to both the resources and the work. Also, in these white circles we can include distractions.

If there was a perfect match between the priorities and the resources, the resources and the 4 P's, the 4 P's to the work, and the 4 P's were 100 percent efficient, then the centre circle would be large (figure 2.1). The reality is that the world is less than perfect. The mismatch between the selected work and its suitability to the resource pool reduces the size of the centre. The efficacy of the 4 P's and their mismatch to the resource pool further reduces the size of the centre (figure 2.2). The better the match between the quality/quantity mix of the resources, the work, and the 4 P's, the more productive the team will be, and the centre circle of the diagram will be larger (figure 2.1).

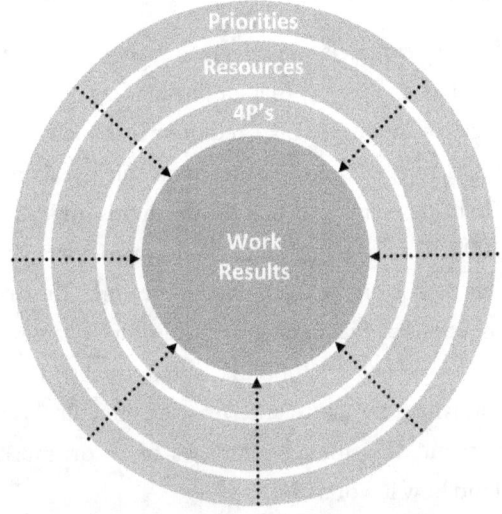

Fig 2.1 The Management Model in a Perfect World

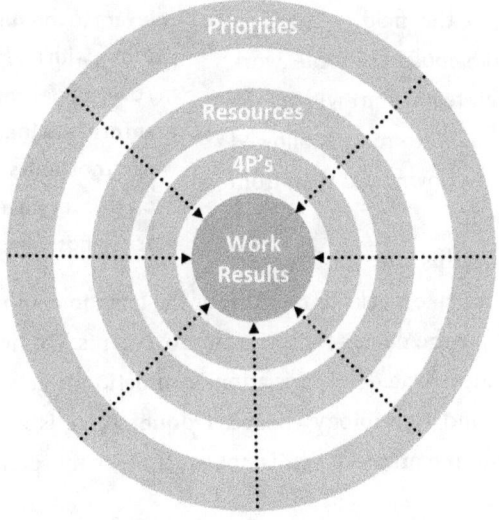

Fig 2.2 The Management Model in the Real World

Looking at the Work

The subject of enterprise architecture is about understanding the work and expressing that understanding in a common convention or language. Like requirements management in chapter 8, the size of this topic is well outside the scope of this book. There are many texts that deal with this subject.

In 2003, I had the pleasure to listen to John Zachman deliver his course on the Zachman Framework. The one thing I remember about that course was the simple statement that this framework helps you think about things. This is the context in which the term "enterprise architecture" is used in this book: building models or views of an organization to understand how it works.

There are many ways to go about understanding the work. Before deciding to hire a consultant in the field, a manager can and should do some work with their team. Start with a look from the bottom up, followed by the top down, and then from the sides.

There are lots of ways to go about developing these views. I explore references relevant to the subject I am working with and then draft my own model and have the team critique them over weeks, not hours. There should never be a rush for these things.

While this can start on day one, it can take weeks or months for the team to comprehend sufficiently the details for major improvements. Do not overlook issues related to legislation, competition, economics, culture, and technology change. I doubt there is a spot in the modern workplace that is not touched by more than one of these.

Bottom-Up View

The bottom-up view starts with the team members' work. Ask them what they do and how and why they do it. The discussion should cover practices, processes, procedures, and policies—not necessarily in that order—to understand how these things impact their work.

These discussions with the team members reveal critical performance issues, problem areas, strengths, and weaknesses. It is also a great place to start relationship building. In the details of these discussions, an understanding of what makes the team members tick should begin to emerge.

Top-Down View

The top-down view starts with what is expected of the team. These are the expectations of the team's superior organization, its clients, and the group itself. These are combined and expressed in the goal, vision, and mission statements for the team.

It is vital to have team participation in developing these statements. Their unforced acceptance and buy-in is a cornerstone of the right culture. Supervising managers should occasionally talk about these statements at team meetings and conduct themselves in a way that is consistent with the words. Eventually, the team will pick up on it and suggest amendments from which a discussion and acceptance will happen.

List the functions necessary to satisfy or at least be consistent with the expectations. Break them down to a task level. Look at the bottom-up view and 4 P's. Resolve or note any discrepancies for future reference. The engagement of the team in the discussion is more important than precision. Precision will develop with time and practice.

Other Views

Teams have interactions with other groups. These groups may be internal or external. Include these relationships here.

Integrating the Views

The objective is to bring all these views together to form a picture of how things work and this, for me, is the value of enterprise architecture activities. It can take months for all the pieces to come together in the right order. Perfection in the integrated view of the work is not necessary. The details will not be right at this stage regardless of the amount of study.

Next Steps

The top-down breakdown and bottom-up processes will meet. The supervising manager brings these two views together to make a work breakdown structure (WBS). A WBS is a decomposition of a task into its component parts. The task can be any size. The decomposition is down to the level that a subordinate package of work is manageable or doable. The granularity of this decomposition is important to efficient execution of the work.

A WBS looks like an inverted tree with no noticeable trunk. The first branches start at ground level. At the end of the branches are the leaves. It is at these leaves that the work exists. Alternately, one might imagine a tree route system with leaves.

If the WBS is too much work for the team, there are two options:

1. Adjust the quality/quantity mix of the team, or

2. Adjust expectations in the vision and mission statements.

In practice, the supervising manager will do some of each.

However, before taking these significant steps, keep in mind that there is always a gap between the expectations coming down and what the resources can actually do going up. The supervising manager works to close the gap by making the team more productive.

The Supervising Manager

Start by adjusting the 4 P's from the bottom up with the practices, then continue with the procedures and processes. These can be small, low-risk changes that test the models and deliver the most quickly felt benefits.

The supervising manager:

– Understands the work from the top down, bottom up, and from the sides.

– Encourages team members and makes them feel comfortable expressing themselves in discussions about the work, its failings, and potential areas of improvement.

– Engages team members to talk informally about their work, what they do, what they like and do not like.

– Moderates and listens to discussions and encourages suggestions about what might fix problems.

– Prepares a plan to address the issues identified by the team. Gets their feedback.

– Genuinely listens to all the feedback on the plan. Provides information and reasoning for the plan. Adjusts as required.

– Never skirts the issue or avoids the discussion.

 Keep in mind two points:

– Leaving things to sit for a while is seldom a bad idea.

– Referential authority—authority based on respect and trust in the competence of an individual that a group gives to that individual—is always the most valuable authority.

 Lastly, it might be helpful to think of work as a bit like a family dinner. Not everybody likes everything on the table. People have different tastes. But they recognize that a particular food might be good for them even though they are not keen on it. Perhaps they will eat it anyway.

– Workplaces have a variety of work to be done.

– Keeping work interesting keeps people interested in working.

– Distribute the tedious work fairly.

– Everyone should have some work that interests them.

– As much as possible, match the tasks to the people and the people to the tasks.

The Work: Key Points

- The culture and the management model develop around the work.

- Understand the work. Like a ball, look at it from all angles.

- Encourage team discussion and do more listening.

- Suggest solutions to problem areas and accept feedback.

- Leaving things to sit for a while is seldom a bad idea.

- Make sure everyone has something that interests them and something not so interesting on their plate.

- Keeping work interesting keeps people interested in working.

BOTTOM LINE: Priorities (the what and why), resources (the who), and the efficacy of the 4 P's (the when, where, why, and how) constrain the work. The better the team understands the answers to these questions, the better their performance will be.

Notes

Chapter 5
ROLE-BASED TEAM STRUCTURES

A characteristic of my best teams was the ability of the team members to switch jobs. My preference was to evolve team members away from jobs and into roles. In a role, they could do many jobs. Role-based teams were more robust and better equipped to deal with a variety of changes that can happen in the workplace. These teams could look at a problem, see what had to be done, and adjust to the change—often in the space of an hour or two.

A good everyday example of a role-based team structure is found in team sports. People are qualified—by virtue of the fact they have the ability—to play a sport. They may have to play more than one position, and they may have to play any of those positions within an overall team playing philosophy and a particular strategy for the team they face.

Like a sports team, people don't walk into a work environment and start playing at a high level. Regardless of the talent a player possesses, they need time to develop through coaching, practice, and matches. In our work environment, this groundwork happens in understanding the work and developing the 4 P's. Our core behaviours influence how successful we will be. This chapter provides some tactics that I found useful when building my teams.

Role-based teams build on a good understanding of the work, which is consistent with the desired culture. In the work environment, we do not want the mindset of "I have a job, this is what I do," and "I do this and only this." We seek an environment where team members are comfortable on the move.

In a role-based structure:

– Role descriptions describe the scope of the work for the role but not the details of how it is performed.

– Team members have areas of responsibility and sufficient freedom to fulfil that responsibility.

Changing things up from time to time freshens the work and the workspace, bringing forward different perspectives and ideas. Different experiences develop a broader individual knowledge and confidence base together, with a healthy attitude to change. Under these conditions a gentle turnover can happen. This contributes to the freshening process. It is not something to be feared, rather embrace it!

For small groups, I was pleased to see an annual personnel turnover of around 5 percent.

A team of such individuals is resilient, more together, better able to adapt to change, and take it in their stride.

It is unrealistic to expect that everyone will be right in every role on a team. That is not the goal. The mini goal here is to build resilience by developing across the team an appreciation of every aspect of the team's work, based on experience, not talk. This approach improves teamwork. On the way, team members will learn things about themselves, and that knowledge does not come free. What might be perceived as a negative or a failure is a potential learning experience.

Forming Team Roles

Team roles must be a good match to the people who perform the work. Look at the work-breakdown structure (chapter 4) and group together the functions to create a suitable role. Team members participate in this process and make recommendations as required. At the end of the process, all tasks—the leaves of the WBS—must be assigned to a role.

The proper development of the roles, and the 4 P's required to execute the work, happen in parallel.

Team Roles: Descriptions

The team role descriptions:

- Cover the scope of the work-breakdown structure but not the details.

- Allow some freedom for people to choose how to do the work.

- Match the talents, tastes, and preferences of the people in the team's recruiting pool.

- Are written at a level of granularity or level of detail that does not require amendment because of changes in work details.

- Allow or facilitate improvements to the work to facilitate incremental change.

- Are described jointly with the people doing the work to understand what is required of them in their own language.

- Cover for absences.

Freshen things up occasionally by swapping assignments or roles once these have been created.

These discussions and the preparation of the role descriptions must happen with complete transparency and involve all concerned. Team members must understand the team roles and their role in the team, agree that the words match the intent, and then act accordingly. The language used must have the same meaning to everyone on the team.

Role-Based Team Structures: Key Points

- Create a role-based organizational structure which allows people a certain level of freedom—in their roles—to do their work.

- Ensure team members understand the team roles and their role in the team.

- If possible, switch the team members in their roles to freshen things up from time to time.

BOTTOM LINE: Role-based teams support a broader knowledge of the work. As a result, the team is more resilient in change.

Notes

Chapter 6
WORK PLANNING

Effective planning of the work is the foundation for results. Absolutely critical to effective work planning is effective priority management. If priority management fails, then the work fails.

Work plans should be living documents that reflect changes and adjustments to changing circumstances. But, if plans change too often, nothing gets done. Plans need to have a time horizon that is right for their purpose. Products for changing markets will have nearer plan horizons than infrastructure projects. Corporate strategic plans have a different planning horizon than the plans for their products.

> I recall a TV documentary on planning in the 1990s, when one of the speakers said, "Plans exist so that when they change, those involved may know what has changed and perhaps why."

Clear work planning is another key part of developing the desired culture, and results won't happen without it.

Work Plans

The supervising manager will likely have several plans:

- For the products they make, the services they provide, or projects they execute.

- At least one for team development, changes, and adjustments.

- For results (chapter 7).

- A development plan for each team member.

If work priorities change every month, there is not a lot of point in a six-month plan. And, if it takes six months to produce or deliver something and the priorities change every month, the plan will not succeed, except by particularly good luck.

The job of the work plan is to guide the team's energy to the work. The more stable the plan is over its planning horizon, the more productive it will be. For this to happen, effective priority management is crucial.

Considerations for a Work Plan

Resource requirements. The planned work should just exceed the resources available. Not everything proceeds smoothly. When a job must unexpectedly stop, the team needs to have alternate work.

Flexibility. Genuine surprises happen where something must be done immediately. Changing a work plan does have a resource cost. Verify that the benefit of changing the plan outweighs its cost.

Planning horizon. Too many genuine surprises make the work plan ineffective. In this case, ask the question: Is the planning horizon correct? If the work becomes too fragmented, productivity will drop, and the organization is in trouble!

Work types. Recognize different work types and allow them to progress. In most organizations, there are larger and smaller packages of work. Some smaller packages of work have a low resource cost but a high value. Look at the work in the organization. If appropriate, have different work plans and paths for different types of packages. This is one way to address the need for flexibility.

Visibility. The work plan must be visible or at least easily accessible to the team. They should be able to read, understand, and follow it. It should show progress against the planned schedule and resource consumption.

Focus. To maintain the team's focus on the priorities, the work plan must reflect those of the organization.

Priority Management

Priority management should feed the work plan by identifying the candidate packages of work for inclusion in the next work planning cycle.

There are two parts to priority management:

1. Gathering the collection of candidate work packages.

2. Choosing the right candidates for the next work planning cycle.

Candidate work packages may come from various sources through processes that evaluate the value of them. Some of the sources are:

– The client(s) or customer(s).

– Organizational, top-down assignments.

– Interfacing internal organizations.

– External organizations.

– The team.

If the work from these sources requires significant effort, this work should be visible in a work plan and not ignored.

Gathering the Collection of Candidate Work Packages

An effective priority management system needs sufficient information to choose which work packages should be in the work plan when the team is not properly employed.

The last of my teams settled on the answers to the five questions posed in chapter 9, "Change Management," relating to background, objective, deficiency, highest-level requirements, and solution expectations. A private sector organization would include criteria such as net present value (NPV) or return on investment (ROI).

The information in the candidate list must be current, and shared editing of the list makes this easier. How this happens depends on the technology tools in use and the size and complexity of the stakeholder groups. Try to avoid the situation where one person receives information updates by email for transcription into the list. At the other extreme, for large groups, not everybody can update the list either. A balanced approach is required.

In figure 5 (chapter 10), priority management is contained in the register of issues and ideas. A register is a table of rows and columns; one item to a row and sufficient columns to capture other relevant information. A spreadsheet can be a register as can a table in a word processor software. A module in the IBM product Rational DOORS may also be a register. This is further discussed in chapter 8, "Requirements Management," and part three, "Route to the Book."

This register contains the information, such as resource and schedule estimates and current work phase, that the work management body uses to monitor the progress of work through all its stages from "we need to do this" through to completion. The information gathered in the priority list is part of the work decision-making process through the entire product or service cycle. The information gathered at the beginning in the priority list is just that—the beginning.

Choosing the Right Candidates for the Next Planning Cycle

When there is space in the work plan, the list is reviewed and an appropriate item is selected.

There are many ways to assess the value of a work package. These range from the detailed methodical analysis to pure gut instinct. The right candidates for the next planning cycle are the ones that, as a package, give the highest net reward for the available resources. Usually, these would be a few must-dos filled in with a selection from the rest. It is important to have the agreement of all stakeholders in the list of candidates for the work plan: consult, discuss, influence, and be influenced, leading to a consensus agreement of all those around or at the table.

Genuine emergency items will not be on the list for long. Things that are on the list for a long time are probably never going to get selected. They should be discarded with an explanation.

It is helpful if the list of priorities is visible or at least easily accessible to support team awareness of priorities to maintain focus. The "priority list" should form part of the information model supporting the work.

Events Register

The work plan provides the numbers for progress but not the "feel." A register of events provides a feel for the progress. The register contains all the events significant to progress a work package.

In the events register, the following details are useful:

– Type of event (meeting, demonstration, conference, and similar events).

– Date.

– Duration.

– Attendees.

– Chair (who called it).

– Objective.

– A brief summary of discussion.

– Action items.

The total content is measured in tens of words, not hundreds. It is helpful if:

– The entries are in reverse chronological order so that the last entry is at the top.

– The event links to its work package in the priority list.

Lastly, if the supervising manager asks questions of the organization from these event records, they will be better maintained (refer to chapter 10, "Communications").

Planning the Work

The value of the team is maximized when it is delivering the best selection of work packages. One plan might fit all. But, if it does not, it is acceptable to have more than one type of work plan. The objective is to have work plans that are stable and productive.

To decide upon the number and type of work plans required, you must understand the work and the things that influence it: markets, work package size, lead time, investment, and other factors.

Selecting the right combination of work packages to fill the plan(s) is critical to maximizing the team's value. To provide the profile of resource use over the planning horizon, add the target completion date and resource information for the work packages. After some debate and experimentation, the final agreed work selection comes together.

Work plans, once established, should be respected as the work progresses. Pauses are forecasted and planned. Temporarily stopping and starting work has a cost. Such decisions require careful consideration.

Even a team that is robust and excellent at adjusting to changes in the work will lose some productivity when a plan changes; however, a team, developing as intended by this book, will quickly adapt, and keep that loss to a minimum. Regardless of the work team's ability, overall failure is still guaranteed if priorities are not sufficiently stable.

Work plans show people the results of their efforts. People like to see their efforts are generating results.

If you are a novice at this activity, don't be alarmed or surprised if your work plan does not work as forecasted. It takes some time and patience to develop the experience, knowledge, and skill to use it correctly. Do not ignore the plan! Work with it, then adjust it to reflect reality as it unfolds. Maintain versions so that you may see the differences between what was forecasted and reality. Think about and note why that difference occurred. You will improve!

Work Planning: Key Points

– Work plans are critical to the communications required to support the development of the culture.

– Work plans guide the available energy to the work.

– Effective work planning maximizes the value of the work.

– Effective work plans have a planning horizon that suit the environment in which they are used.

– The nature of an organization's priorities and how they change is a factor in the mix when determining a planning horizon.

– Priority management is a crucial component of work planning.

– Effective priority management is critical to maximizing the value of the work and supporting stable plans.

BOTTOM LINE: Effective planning of the work is the foundation for results and an enabler for the culture.

Notes

Chapter 7
RESULTS

The previous chapters were about laying the groundwork to get results by tapping into team energy and using that energy wisely through an appropriate management model. Results do not just happen with a work plan; they must be achieved. There must be something in effect that moves the team toward the desired results. The last essential component to tapping into that team energy is active, results-oriented management.

It is my experience that results-oriented working must be part of the team culture. The team must understand that the work plan describes what they should be working on in a time frame, while the results plan(s) tells them what they need to accomplish next.

Traditionally there are two basic methods, each with a few variants on the theme.

Method 1 is the progress chaser.

- Someone is tasked to keep track of the work and accomplishes this by disturbing the work to ask questions.

- A variant of this is the supervising manager who cannot resist being a progress chaser.

Method 2 is the progress report.

- Team members prepare the report.

- The report is incorrectly or poorly completed.

- Poorly completed or not, the report is then more or less ignored in favour of method 1 above.

Notwithstanding that office technology has rendered both methods 1 and 2 obsolete, they are alive and well in some and perhaps many workplaces. Technology can be a tool to show both methods the exit door; however, there are at least three prerequisites that must be met before a technology tool can do that.

- A supervising manager with the right vocabulary (chapter 1). They know what information is required to evaluate a need for their intervention based on what is happening in the work environment and the consequences of letting it play out.
- A disciplined team to document the information required.
- A disciplined manager to review the information without interrupting the work.

The point is simply this: a disciplined team—including the manager—that is aware of its responsibilities, the information required, and the relative importance of the work, does not need progress chasing! It succeeds at results management.

Results Plans

Results plans target work packages, individuals, or both. Results plans' cycles are short when compared to a work plan horizon. If a work plan horizon is one year, the results plan cycle might be measured in months or quarters of a year. In the software industry, "agile" development has a results cycle measured in hours.

Establishing the Results

The results that are set should try to stretch individuals but not overwhelm or break them. It is an inexact process.

1. Review the work plan to ensure that each package has an office of primary interest (OPI; the person or organization that is responsible for the work package) who knows everything there is to know about said work package.

2. In conjunction with the work package OPI, determine the next required result and the target date or time frame (the cycle) for it to be achieved.

3. During the cycle, monitor what is going on and judge the need for intervention. If people are struggling, the manager should recognize this and act on the mentoring opportunity.

4. At the end of the cycle, assess performance against the target. It is nonsense that targets must be measurable. A qualitative assessment can be quite satisfactory.

5. Discuss and set the targets for the next cycle.

This is a learning exercise for the manager and the individuals as they explore strengths and weaknesses. Result targets should improve with every cycle. To be clear, it is not about lowering the bar; it is about setting the bar at the right height for team and individual development and growth.

You should program more results than the available resources can achieve because:

– Progress to some of these targets will be impeded by factors outside of the team's control.

– Team members should have some choice and discretion in their work. This encourages thinking about the work.

Monitoring Results

Some of the ways a supervising manager can monitor results follow below. Each of these ways must be aligned and consistent with the work plan. They cannot be divergent.

Work review meetings. These meetings require an effective results plan to guide the discussion and an effective chairperson to keep them moving to schedule.

– Everyone in the meeting is either a person who knows exactly what is going on with a work package (OPI) or a person who is impacted or has a stake in the work package (office of collateral interest, OCI).

– Every work package must be reviewed.

– Meeting frequency depends on the work. It can be daily in an agile environment; in other settings, perhaps weekly or monthly.

– If there is a sense that everything is working well and there is nothing to say, then cancel the meeting.

– If it often happens that two or more meetings in a row are cancelled, perhaps the scheduled meetings are too frequent.

Events register. The events register (chapters 6 and 10) is the diary of significant events for every work package. The length of an entry is measured in tens of words, not hundreds.

Periodically scan this register to get a feel for progress and assess the need for intervention. It is often a source of good questions that lead to valuable answers.

Team meetings. Team meetings cover all the issues that impact the team and the work. These meetings provide mentoring and learning opportunities to better understand the work environment and why it must be that way.

Maintain an open-door policy. This policy refers to a state of mind that indicates that the manager is approachable. They will make time to discuss issues that are bothering a team member.

It takes work and energy to be constructively receptive all or most of the time. It is better to choose a time when energy levels are good. An open-door policy is a crucial tool in relationship building; all concerned need to be mindful of how it is used.

Discussions should focus on progress or attempts to progress the work and seek inputs on ideas that can multiply the work done, solve a problem, or remove a problematic barrier.

Management by walking about. Taking a few minutes of the day to stroll around the team's work domain can provide a good feel about how things are going.

One of my bosses reckoned he could tell how the factory was working as he walked through it in the morning. This was true for all my teams throughout my professional life.

– Engage team members in their work setting.

– Informal discussions about matters other than work improve the manager's accessibility.

– If there is something to say about work, it will come out naturally.

Performance reviews; meetings with individuals. For our purposes, the reviewing of performance is a process to encourage individual growth and development. It has at least three one-on-one sessions: beginning, middle and end of cycle.

Beginning. Discuss and agree on performance objectives for the coming year—the plan. Anywhere from six to eight objectives is a good number. These should be a mix of work plan results and broader items to develop knowledge or skill.

Middle. Review progress against the plan. Some items progress entirely satisfactorily. Others are halted by circumstances outside of the team member's control. These require adjustments to the plan. Lastly, there are the problematic items. Discuss these so that the team member sees a way ahead and what needs to be done for success.

End. The last meeting evaluates the progress made against each objective. There should not be any surprises at this meeting.

Developing performance objectives is a skill. Like all skills, it takes practice. A good performance objective:

– Is clear, concise, and unambiguous.

– Has clear and assessable criteria for success.

– Challenges but does not overwhelm the individual.

– Is accepted by the individual.

Discussion and trust are key. It is a mentoring process that contributes to building supportive relationships. An open and receptive attitude in both parties is required. Team members should find their way to succeed; however, and as a last resort, if someone is truly stopped, that person should not be expected or allowed to spin their wheels and go nowhere.

Supervising managers do not stand around and watch a failure occur; they engage, identify the problem, and guide the individual to success.

Results: Key Points

– Results don't just happen, they are targeted and achieved.

– A work planning cycle will contain many results planning cycles.

– Interaction between the supervising manager and the team is a must.

– There are several tactics available which can work separately or together. They must be consistent and aligned, not divergent.

  · Work review meetings.

  · Events register.

  · Team meetings.

  · Maintaining an open-door policy.

  · Management by walking around.

  · Performance reviews; meetings with individuals.

BOTTOM LINE: Results are achieved by setting reasonable targets and maintaining focus in all team interactions.

Notes

Chapter 8
REQUIREMENTS MANAGEMENT

Requirements management is involved in every aspect of the workplace. It underpins:

- The work in all its forms: project, program, service, or product.

- Performance assessments in all their forms: individual, team, contract, project, program, product, and service.

- Procurements in all their forms: erasers to spaceships and huge construction projects and everything in between.

I am not suggesting for one minute that everyone needs to document their requirements all the time. But, if there is a problem with something you are doing or buying, think about requirements. If the first question you ask yourself is "what is the work," the second question is "what are the requirements?"

Requirements describe something that is needed. It is how a client tells a solution provider the performance objectives of the thing they need or want. Like all performance objectives, they should be assessable.

The relationship between the client and solution provider influences the level of assessability. A legally binding relationship might be different than an internal agreement between two parts of the same organization.

Think of requirements as a means to convey an understanding of the subject. When combined with the effective change management of requirements this thinking can facilitate:

– The right type of relationship between client and solution provider.

– Issue resolution.

Requirements Express What Is Needed or Wanted

Requirements describe something you want or need. The usual form can include sentences or paragraphs, often arranged as a list, which may also have subordinate requirements. Each list item refers to something you want or need the thing to do. A simple example would be "a car is required." It could also be "a social services centre is required" or perhaps a sports centre. Taking the first example as the one most people are familiar with, as written, it could be any car. If the requirement is for any car, then that is the end of it.

Suppose any car will not do. The subordinate requirements might be:

– The vehicle shall be capable of carrying four passengers.

– The vehicle shall have one cubic metre of cargo space.

– The vehicle shall be able to travel 600 km between fuel stops.

– The vehicle fuel shall be gasoline or alternately the vehicle shall be electric powered.

– The vehicle shall maintain a speed of 80 km/hr on a 7 percent uphill grade with a passenger and cargo load of 400 kg.

These examples happen to be short sentences. They would be longer if it was necessary, for example, to add more details about passenger size or how the cargo space might be used.

The important point is that a set of requirements should describe what you want or need to the desired level of detail. It might start with a broad statement that is then broken down into component parts through one or more levels to arrive at a set of paragraphs that deal with the specifics.

It helps if the specifics are criteria against which success may be assessed. In our example, can the vehicle carry 400 kg up a 7 percent grade and maintain a speed of 80 km/hr? It may also be helpful to know the rationale, source, or provenance for the requirement. A little context can provide clarity. If a requirement is not specific, any option in that area is possible. The above example did not specify the type of car roof. You might end up with a hard-top or a soft-top or no-top! If that would be a problem, then add a requirement for the roof type to the list. The same thing might apply to the fuel grade or wheel sizes. If a requirement is not specified, you might receive a surprise, and such surprises are not usually positive!

While the example above is for a common product, the principles remain the same regardless of product or service type.

There is a trade-off in the number of requirements used to describe the thing that is needed or wanted. Too few requirements mean that you will not likely get what you want or need, and you will not be satisfied. Too many requirements demand additional valuable or limited resources to determine if the requirements have been satisfied. Too many requirements might also unduly restrict the solution options to the point where there is no affordable solution in the desired time frame. Compromise may be required.

To manage a compromise, the idea that requirements can have various titles that soften the need is popular. A non-mandatory requirement is an oxymoron. Whichever way you look at it, a non-mandatory requirement is an option, not a requirement. Options should improve the value of a solution over one that simply meets the requirement.

What appears as an easy task can quickly get quite complicated. The discipline of requirements engineering has evolved to deal with this complexity. There are several descriptions for requirements engineering on the Internet. In this book, it is intended to mean establishing, documenting, and maintaining requirements in the broader sense and not limited to an engineering process. You do not have to be an engineer or a software specialist to establish, document, and maintain requirements; however, if requirements are a major part of your work, a course is recommended.

Requirements Support Healthy Relationships

Unless you are building your own product or service there is a relationship between the client and a solution provider. The nature of this relationship can be wide and varied in its forms. The relationship can be based on simple trust right through to a legally binding contract.

When it comes to these relationships, requirements can be problematic. A requirements tree starts with the highest requirement: the "I need a car" example above. This high requirement is then broken down or organized into smaller or subordinate more manageable requirements, much like a work breakdown structure (chapter 3). Requirements show an understanding of the work. They transmit that understanding between the client and the solution provider.

If the process continues down to a much smaller level of detail, a requirements statement will evolve into a specification statement. Where one transitions to the other is always a grey zone.

Requirements statements and specification statements are closely related. Client organizations should focus on requirements. Solution providers develop specifications, and they should focus on that part of the work. Here is a potential problem area. It is not uncommon for clients to want to tell solution providers what the specifications should be and for solution providers to tell clients what their requirements should be. A dialogue on the subject to aid understanding is a good thing. Continuing the dialogue indefinitely is a very irritating behaviour and should be avoided at all costs. Clients should not design by requirements and solution providers should not tell clients how to do their job—PERIOD!

When a client is deciding upon what it is they want, it is helpful to have people with recent experience delivering similar products in the team. They know what is within reasonable reach. They also provide a different view on the meaning of the same words in a requirement. This helps to make a requirement clear and not ambiguous.

Understanding develops as the process progresses. It is an error to think that requirements should be fixed. They should not be fluid, but they should be adjustable to accommodate at least the following issues:

- Soft issues that are difficult to express or cannot be
  practically expressed at the outset. These may put pressure
  on the work team and
  impact what is needed.
  Such issues may be
  political or relate to a
  topic that has a lot of
  unknowns in it.

- A revision of the understanding that will most
  likely develop over time
  through the work to
  explore the subject.

> A good example of something
> loaded with unknowns, political
> requirements, and a developing
> understanding would be President
> Kennedy's declaration that the US
> would put a man on the moon by
> the end of the decade (the 1960s).
> Another example might be our
> current struggles with climate
> change. Is there any agreement on
> the top-level requirement?

- Changes to the environment in which the product or
  service operates.

- Technological evolution, adjusting the reach of what
  is possible.

Except in simple cases, a list of requirements should never
be considered complete until the work is finished, and the
product or service delivered. If there is poor requirement
discipline during the work process, very often the distinction
between requirement and specification becomes cloudy and
confused. The relationship between the client and the solution provider will be negatively impacted, causing the end
product to suffer.

Throughout the entire solution delivery process, requirements should be the ever-present beacon that maintains the
team's work focus. For that to happen, they must be accurate
and reflect any changes as they occur. In the "good fences

make good neighbours" proverb, requirements can and should be the fence that manages what are the clients' and solution providers' respective spheres of responsibility, regardless of the nature of their relationship.

Changes in requirements happen. The question is when to implement them. This is a value proposition: the cost of not adopting the change versus the cost of the change. Some things to think about in this situation:

– Requirement changes that have no impact on the scope of work, budget, or schedule are usually accommodated without issue.

– Requirement changes that impact the scope of work, budget, or schedule can be more problematic, particularly if the impact is an increase in the budget or a lengthening of the schedule.

How these issues are resolved depends on the value propositions that apply to the client and the solution provider. Is it a formal contract between two arm's length entities, or are they part of the same organization? While an interesting negotiating problem, it is not relevant to the goal of this book.

All we need to understand is that:

– Requirements may change and why they might change.

– Not all changes will be adopted.

– Requirements delineate the sphere of responsibilities between the client and the solution provider.

– For good team performance, the information relating to requirements needs to be open to all team members to guide their work.

- The relationship between a client and a solution provider can easily sour when expectations are not met or appear threatened. There are many potential reasons for this, but requirements do not have to be one of them.

- The requirements change management process facilitates requirements as a flexible fence.

Requirements Change Management

Version control is usually associated with documents or software products. Requirements change management is version control applied to a requirements statement. It is the process by which a requirements statement is amended, adjusted, changed, added, or deleted.

A Simple but Powerful Model

Figure 3 is a simple but powerful information model to manage requirements change that can be implemented using desktop spreadsheet or database technologies for small work packages. A more sophisticated tool, like IBM's Rational DOORS, is needed for complex and larger work packages. The implementation details will depend on the software in use.

There are three registers in the model:

- The client requirements register.

- The work-in-progress requirements register.

- The issues register.

These registers contain records that include any needed or wanted attributes. Keep in mind that information has a cost. Only add the attributes that the work demands. Less is best.

Referring to figure 3, the implementation steps are:

1. Create the client requirements register and the issues register in the software product you use.

2. Document the client requirements.

3. Record issues that arise in documenting the requirement in the issue register and link to the requirement. When all the issues are resolved amongst the stakeholders, the client requirements are complete.

4. Copy the client requirement register to create the work-in-progress register.

5. Link the records in the client requirements register to their corresponding records in the work-in-progress register.

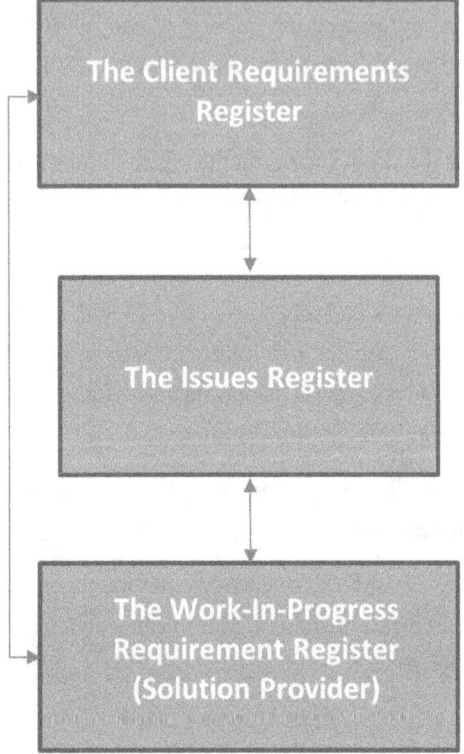

Fig 3 Requirements Change Management Model

The requirements in the work-in-progress register guide the current work in whatever form it takes.

Why are there two registers of requirements? In every case, the environment always changes before the work-in-progress. It always leads the work; it must. There is no possible alternative. The client requirements always lead the work in progress. Trying to track the changes of both in one register generates fog.

Using the Model

An issue with a requirement in the work-in-progress requirements register. It would normally be the solution provider who first becomes aware of this and raises the issue by making the entry describing the issue in the issues register. The client may also raise an issue that they become aware of. A change in the understanding of the work would be the cause of such a change.

An issue with a requirement in the client requirements register. This register tracks what is happening in the environment into which the solution will be delivered. If there is a change in this register, it would normally be the client who raises the issue and makes the entry describing the issue in the issues register.

Entering the issue in the issues register. Once the issue is entered in the register, it is linked to the relevant requirements in both the work-in-progress and client requirements registers.

Deciding on the issue. Reviewers will do the background research work required by the issue's complexity, entering their notes on important points. They may or may not make a recommendation on accepting the change in requirements. These reviews can happen in parallel or sequentially. Once the reviews and comments are added, the required approvals can be given or withheld if the value proposition does not support approval.

Historical record. It is important for the client to keep track of what is happening in the target environment over the course of the work. When the work is finished, it most likely will not provide 100 percent satisfaction to the client and the client will need to understand the difference between that which is a result of changes in their environment and that which is due to contract performance. Changes in the client requirements register reflect changes in the environment. Changes in the work-in-progress requirements register reflect changes in the contracted work.

This approach provides a living record of the client requirements of the work and the requirements for the work in progress. It is a flexible but robust fence between client requirements and the contracted work of the solution provider.

At some point during the work, the sum of the differences between client requirements and contracted requirements may provide a value proposition to update the contract for the work in execution.

– A modification to the work in progress and its scope, cost, and schedule parameters reduces or eliminates the divergence between the two tables/registers.

– It may also generate a new work package starting with two identical tables.

The model supports the need for timely management action and suppresses distractions and work eddies that detract from team efficiency. In addition,

– The supervising manager may quickly notice the degree of divergence and assess the need for a timely intervention.

– New hires can quickly see why some things are done one way or another.

– All can see when an issue was raised and why it remains unresolved. Is it time to raise it again?

Requirements: Issues Resolution

When the solution provider and client are satisfied that the product or service is as ordered, the client decides whether to put it into service. During the build process, it is possible that a change in the target environment impacted the solution's effectiveness such that once the product is in service it does not meet the end user's needs.

Examining the requirements and their attached notes should provide a detailed diary of every decision made about a requirement. An objective assessment about what happened should be doable. The assessment might be clearer compared to not examining the requirements and having a discussion based on recollections supported by selected emails and the like. Additionally, it may be easier and quicker to determine the impact, scope of work, cost, and schedule for the adjustments necessary to make it right.

At the very least, there is a lesson to be observed and maybe learned.

Requirements Management: Key Points

- Requirements describe something you want or need.

- The level of detail and assessment of a requirement are influenced by the relationship between a client and their solution provider.

- In the "good fences make good neighbours" proverb, requirements are the fence between a client and their solution provider.

- Requirements work stops when the work is complete and not before.

- Changes to requirements do happen. Plan to adjust or change written requirements during the process, or plan to fail.

- Effective requirement change management influences the relationship between client and solution provider.

- Should things start to go wrong in the work, a focus on requirements can defuse situations.

BOTTOM LINE: Requirements show an understanding of the work and support the communication of that understanding between those wanting the work completed (the client) and those doing the work (the solution provider).

Notes

Chapter 9
CHANGE MANAGEMENT

Discussion and team interaction is a common theme in the environment. Ideas and suggestions come from this dialogue and should be harvested in a risk-managed way. Change management brings this to the table. It is a non-discretionary part of the environment.

Over the years, I have been exposed to many change processes. The approach I favour—it is the most successful I have seen in use—is the subject of this chapter.

Change actions can relate to anything, and depending on the change, the associated artifacts are different. Artifacts are the range of things to implement a change that are constructed by people, which for the purposes of this book includes a service. Change management is seldom easy, and it is quite understandable why many people do not like change. The more a change can be seen as the natural evolution of things, the more likely the change will be successful. Evolution does not have to be at the cadence of a geologic clock.

The need for a change, whether internal or external to the organization, or product related, starts with the idea that something is perhaps not right or could be better. To take this further, the thought needs to be expressed to assess its validity and practicability. In these two sentences, there are three problem areas:

1. The ever-present "good idea" that is anything but.

2. Clarity. Very often, the way in which an idea is expressed has different meanings to different people.

3. Resources—always scarce—should be committed to good cases for change.

Five Questions to Ask

The answers to the following five questions provide a simple, understandable approach to describing a change. The answers develop a common understanding across the team, exposing the weak good idea early on, providing some assurance that only the good cases for change get the valuable resources. This information should be recorded in the register of issues and Ideas.

What Is the Background?

Before jumping to a conclusion about a "deficiency," take a moment to consider the context of what you think is weak or to be improved. There is not a fixed set of boxes to be checked. Answering the following questions may help you put together the picture.

– What is the topic of interest? Is it part of something larger? What is its history?

– Who uses the thing or the larger object?

– Where is it used? This does not necessarily mean a physical location; it could also be part of a process.

– When is it used? Continuously, regularly, etc.?

- Why is it used? What is the purpose of the thing or the larger object, and why is this purpose essential?

- How is the thing or larger object used?

- Is there a suggestion on how to improve upon the weakness?

- How would the suggestion impact the answers to the questions, what, who, where, when, why, and how?

What Is the Objective?

If a deficiency exists, then there must be an objective to which it relates. It is not the objective of the change in mind but the original objective of the work or business function to which the deficiency relates. Beware of the deficiency that cannot be expressed relative to the objective to which it should refer!

What Is the Deficiency?

How does the topic you have noticed impede the attainment of the end objective? Stating a solution option, "I need a car (because I do not have one)" is not a deficiency. A deficiency might be, "I cannot accept a particular job because *I cannot get to the required place on time.*" There are several options to solve this problem, one of which may be a car.

What Are the Highest-Level Requirements?

What are the top-level requirements that will satisfy the original objective?

What Do You Expect the
Solution to Look Like?

When there is a recognition that a deficiency exists, there is usually an idea of what could address the issue.

The answers to these five questions might seem to come easily at first. Each of the answers must make sense when read with the answers to the other four questions. It can be an iterative process. Introducing other people with alternate views will generate further work on the answers. Eventually, the agreement reached on the answers to these five questions indicates a common understanding of the issue. The next step is to evaluate the business benefit and where it might fit in the work plan.

Managing Change Work

A risk-managed approach to change work avoids the premature or over-commitment of resources (figure 4). In this six-stage process, the change is explored one stage at a time. The end of a stage is a gate. To pass through a gate, a team must provide the information detailed in the "Change Stages" section of this chapter. This content should suit the project and be defined in deliverables.

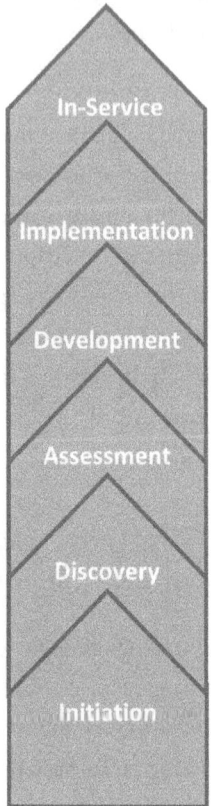

Fig 4 Change Process

Risks are highest at the bottom of the diagram, where detailed information about the change is scarce. This process works regardless of the size of the change. For a small change, the process may take minutes. For large changes, it can take years.

The first three stages (initiate, discovery, and assessment) are the "thinking about it" phase. In these stages, the resource commitment is small relative to the last three stages (development, implementation, and in-service) that comprise the "doing it" phase.

At the end of assessment, many but not all risks should be exposed and assessed. Measures to mitigate the identified risks are acted upon as early as is reasonably possible. The use of "should" is intentional because risks can reveal themselves anywhere in the process.

The question for each stage in the thinking phase is how far should the analysis go? With more work, it follows that estimates on cost and schedule should become increasingly accurate as the process proceeds. There are three ("thinking about it") stages, so three levels or classes of the estimate are needed. I use the labels "budget," "indicative," and "substantive." Next, decide the limits on the estimate for each of the labels. Several factors can come into play—for example:

> I found the following classes of estimate worked well. Other levels can be used to suit the organizational requirement.
> -Initiate Stage: budget estimate, plus or minus 50 percent.
> -Discovery Stage: indicative estimate, plus or minus 20 percent.
> -Assessment Stage: substantive estimate, plus or minus 10 percent.

– How risk-averse is the organization?

– Is the business inherently risky?

– How much control is required over the solution?

Considering only cost and schedule as the gate criteria can place you in the right area, but this may not be sufficient. It is not hard and fast. Do the work necessary to be sufficiently comfortable about moving on to the next stage (refer to the section on "Change Stages" later in this chapter to get a better idea of what is meant here). It is tough to be totally or completely comfortable. There is nearly always some risk. Plans seldom survive first engagement unless the situation is straightforward. Be prepared to adapt to the reality, whatever that may be.

Use the requirements (chapter 8) as the backbone to guide the exploratory work and keep it on topic. Develop the requirements sufficiently to arrive at the level of accuracy required for the estimate at that phase. This work progressively exposes unknowns and risks as the depth of the analysis advances.

Think of requirements as mini performance objectives. They speak to what something must do, and not how it does it. That is the theory. In practice, every organization has a way in which it works. It speaks to the culture of that organization. Organizations use requirements to express how they work. The reality is that requirements express what is needed, and to a limited degree, how that should be delivered. if the requirements are over specified, this will not likely result in the best solution.

To pass through the gate to the next stage, the current stage's deliverables are reviewed and accepted. The list of deliverables is not exhaustive and should be amended as required to meet the circumstances. If an unacceptable risk or problem arises, the work is stopped at that time.

The end of assessment marks the end of thinking about it. The development step is the first of the "doing it" stages. At this juncture, the mindset needs to change from "thinking about it" to a vigorous, but not reckless, prosecution of the change.

In the "thinking about it" phase, the client leads the effort.

They should be thinking about what they are trying to improve, what they want to do, what level of risk to accept, how much they want to pay for the solution, and how long they want it to take. The client will likely need input from people with expertise in delivering the solution (the solution provider).

In the "doing it" phase, the emphasis on leading and driving the work should shift to the solution provider, with the client organization adjusting to an oversight and perhaps active supporting role. How the client and solution provider interact is governed by the agreement between them.

The development stage is where the artifacts of the solution are constructed. The cost to exit increases the deeper into the phase and often quite steeply.

All these steps occur for every single change, even the simplest ones.

Change Stages

Stage 1: Initiation

The resource requirements for the initiation stage should not be large. The overall aim is not to define the solution, but to consider how big the task might be. What should the size of the budget be, and what are the options and risks involved? This work requires some familiarity with the nature of the objectives of this phase. Keeping together a small team of people with the knowledge and experience for initiate analysis-type work is a good thing.

At the end of this stage, the team:

- Adjusts the answers to the five questions, as necessary.

- Recommends the change's objective. The objective must be within the capability of the reasonably available staff.

- Describes the scope of the change.

- Identifies the areas of the business that the change will impact.

- Proposes the options to explore in the discovery phase.

- Develops the budget estimate for cost and schedule.

- Recommends the resource and time allocation for the discovery stage work.

- Recommends the resource and time allocation for the assessment stage work.

- Provides an initial risk assessment.

The information prepared in this stage of the change process should not be large. It should be easily reviewable and accepted by the following people before the discovery stage begins:

- The representatives of the stakeholders in the change, and

- The managers who will commit the resources for the next and later stages in the change process.

Stage 2: Discovery

To proceed further in the process requires the assignment of resources, which means the work is inserted into the work plan.

The discovery stage is in the "thinking about it" phase to explore the requirement more deeply, develop options, and develop indicative estimates for cost and schedule. The work also confirms the size of the change, the impacts, and risks. Exposed risks or errors in the budget estimates might mean stopping the change.

At the end of this stage, the team:

– Adjusts the answers to the five questions, as necessary.

– Confirms or modifies the objective for the change.

– Describes the work to make the change and drafts the statement of work or task statement.

– Updates the impact analysis.

– Recommends the options for evaluation in the assessment phase.

– Develops the indicative estimates for cost and schedule.

– Adjusts the resource requirements and the plan for the assessment phase.

– Updates the initial risk assessment as needed.

The information prepared in this stage of the change process will have increased in relation to the initiate stage. It should still be manageable. Before the assessment stage begins, it needs to be reviewed and accepted by the representatives of the stakeholders in the change and the managers who will commit the resources for the next and later stages in the change process.

Stage 3: Assessment

The assessment stage is the last of the "thinking about it" phases.

The objective is to describe what the product or service must do and how it will be assessed. The desired level of detail in this work is determined by the amount of control the client wants to exert over the solution and the resources available to monitor it. The requirements (chapter 8) describe the product or service.

At the end of this stage, the team:

– Adjusts the answers to the five questions, as necessary.

– Confirms or modifies the objective for the change.

– Develops the requirements, as a minimum, to a level of detail needed to prepare substantive cost estimates for cost and schedule and completes the statement of requirement.

– Describes the work required to make the change and completes the statement of work or task statement.

– Completes the impact analysis.

– Completes the options analysis and recommends an option for the solution.

– Clearly describes the option to provide a common understanding to all stakeholders.

– Provides the substantive estimate for cost and schedule.

– Provides a resourced and scheduled work break-down structure.

– Updates the risk assessment as needed.

Once development starts, the cost of taking an off-ramp goes up quite quickly. To agree that the change is ready to move from "thinking about it" to "doing it," the managers involved must be sufficiently comfortable with the assessment stage results and their ability to support the proposed schedule.

Stage 4: Development

The artifacts are built during the development stage in this change process. The step ends when the artifacts are ready for delivery.

When are the artifacts ready for delivery? One might think this would be when the requirements as stated at the end of the assessment stage are satisfied. Unfortunately, this is not necessarily the case (see preceding chapter on requirements management). The work should be complete when the contract or agreement between the client and solution provider is satisfied. Unfortunately, this does not always mean that the artifacts are ready for delivery.

For a product or service to be ready for delivery, both the client and solution provider should be confident that it will do a good job. Confidence comes from the successful demonstrations, testing, and trials that are appropriate to the industry.

Effective requirements management improves the probability of a successful outcome for this work.

Stage 5: Implementation

Implementation activities are specific to an industry and are outside the scope of this book.

Three things can improve the acceptance of most changes:

1.   A champion in the target environment.

2.   On-topic messaging to emphasize that the change
     has arrived.

3.   Choosing a friendly environment for the early adopters
     to fix issues and avoid early negativity, which can quickly
     turn to failure.

Stage 6: Closure

Closing a change can be challenging. People often want to
move on to the next thing.

It is better to monitor the impact of the change during
the first few months of widespread use to see if the projected
benefits are fully or somewhat achieved. How does what was
supplied compare to what was requested?

If expectations were not met, try to understand why, and
then assess the value proposition of the correction. Effective
requirements management can make this assessment
more manageable.

Finally, it is essential to ensure that records *that will be*
referred to in the future are updated. The important words
here are "that will be." There is no point in updating records
that will not likely be used again.

Change Management: Key Points

–   To build a healthy team, it is especially important to
     encourage ideas, suggestions, and dialogue, and then act
     upon them.

– A change starts with the idea that something is wrong or could be better.

– To describe the change, answer the following questions:

  · What is the background?

  · What is the deficiency?

  · What is the objective?

  · What are the highest-level requirements?

  · What do you expect the solution to look like?

– An incremental and gated approach allows risk-managed progress with a formal off-ramp at the end of each stage.

  · Initiation. How big is the task? What should the budget and timeframe be? What are the options and risks involved?

  · Discovery. Develop the options to indicative estimates of cost and schedule. Confirm the answers to the questions in the initiation section.

  · Assessment. Develop the preferred option(s) to substantive estimates of cost and schedule. Confirm the answers to the questions in the initiation section. Describe what the product or service must do and how it will be assessed.

  · Development. Build the product or service.

  · Implementation. This is industry specific.

  · Closure. Evaluate any gap in expectations and what to do about it. Separate records required for future use from those that will not be required.

- The first three stages (initiate, discovery, and assessment) are the "thinking about it" phase.

- The last three stages (development, implementation, and in-service) are the "doing it" phase, where the change is actively and vigorously prosecuted.

- Effective requirements management supports a satisfactory outcome for both the client and the solution provider.

BOTTOM LINE: Change management is a non-discretionary and critical piece of the management framework.

Notes

Chapter 10
COMMUNICATIONS

Over the past forty years, communication issues have changed considerably. Communication problems used to be related to a lack of information or a lack of access to it. Modern tools seem to have turned that problem on its head. Today, people can prepare and distribute information in a fraction of the time it used to take, but it still takes time to sift through all the material available. The issue is still a lack of (the right) information or lack of access to it, although the cause is completely different.

The model in this chapter (figure 5) supports the better understanding and focus on what information is needed for the work.

Email, text, and the like are great tools that are suited to those aspects of work that don't follow a particular pattern. However, when it comes to team-working, they are very inefficient ways to share information.

Understanding the work means the type of information required to do the job is known. The better the understanding of the work, the better the understanding of the information required to do the work. The team builds their information model and then uses it to keep the information they need to do the work. Having defined what they need, they also know what they don't use. Information that is used is always up to date. The result is an improvement in productivity through improved access to good information.

This model (figure 5) binds the content of the previous nine chapters and provides a backbone for communications through the team. It happens as a function of the work and not a separate, resource-wasting activity.

– Team members know the information that is needed to do the work.

– Team members do not provide information that is not required.

– The risk of distraction by side issues is mitigated.

– Access to needed information is improved.

– Information accuracy is improved because it relates to the work in real-time.

– Clarity and awareness are improved because all the relevant information is in one area. Consequently, the possibility of misunderstandings is reduced.

The information model is a mix of data and documents. Therefore, the information repository is a database and a document repository with version control.

Not all documents are treated the same. Those of a more permanent nature that are part of the solution, such as the 4 P's or corporate records, are treated differently to those of a more temporary nature, such as most but not all emails. The former group will require some form of standardized folder structure and version control. Control applied to that latter group is more relaxed. The point is simply this: give some thought to how documents will be stored and managed. One size does not fit all!

Some implementation points to keep in mind:

– Everyone on the team needs to be clear on the information they need to do their work—including the supervising manager.

– If required information is overlooked or omitted, accept the error, correct it, and move on. This model will have a dynamic component. Accommodating oversights and errors is a fact of life.

– Content must be focused—clear, concise, and complete.

– Documents include all the products of the office automation suite. Such documents are held in a shared file structure. Not on individual drives and email accounts. For success, this is a firmly applied rule. Anything less renders the information model useless.

– Supervising managers must use the model and not bypass it for their work.

The precise information model required will depend on the circumstance; however, the one in figure 5 worked well for my last team.

An Information Model

The information model (figure 5) has two high-level requirements:

1. Guide the scope and critical parameters of the work.

2. Report progress and performance.

The six registers in figure 5 have the following functions:

– Issues and ideas (chapters 6 and 9). Describes the work at a high level, establishes priority in the work plan, and contains timeline as well as resource allocation details.

– Client requirements (chapter 8). Describes the detailed product or service requirements.

– Work packages (chapter 6). Describes the selected performance parameters—for example, cost and schedule—for each work package.

– Events (chapter 7 and 10). This is the record of meetings, presentations, project demonstrations, and so on, relevant to the direction and progress of the work.

– Work-in-progress requirements (chapter 8). Describes the detailed definition of what can be delivered by the work package.

– Issues (chapter 8). Explains the real time differences between the client and solution requirements.

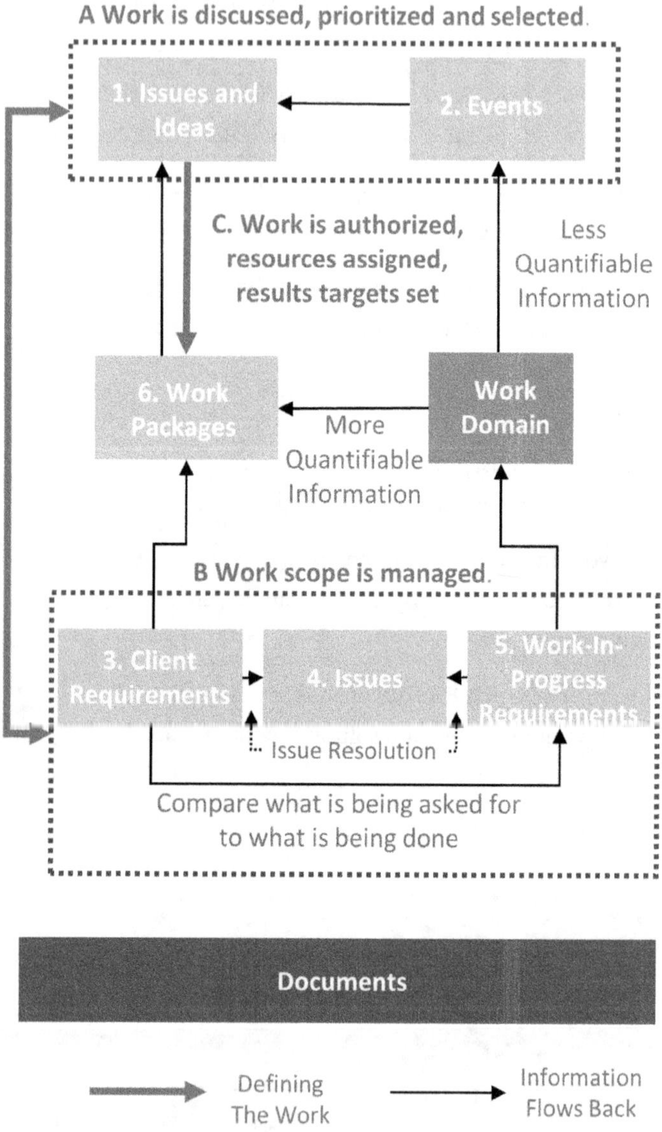

A Work is discussed, prioritized and selected.

| 1. Issues and Ideas | ← | 2. Events |

C. Work is authorized, resources assigned, results targets set

Less Quantifiable Information

| 6. Work Packages | ← More Quantifiable Information | Work Domain |

B Work scope is managed.

| 3. Client Requirements | → 4. Issues ← | 5. Work-In-Progress Requirements |

Issue Resolution

Compare what is being asked for to what is being done

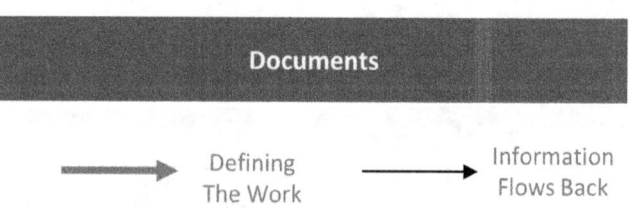

Documents

→ Defining The Work   → Information Flows Back

Fig 5 Information Model

The work starts and ends in the top left corner of the diagram with the register of issues and ideas (1). This is where the work plan starts. As part of that work planning process, there are meetings, demonstrations, and the like on items in the issue and ideas register. These are events.

The events register (2) tends to capture the softer, important, and non-quantifiable information on work items.

Model Flow

Once the decision has been made to include an item in the work plan, work on the client requirements starts. Referring to chapter 8, this work is done in the client requirements register (3) and issues register (4). The process can follow the change management process in chapter 9. When the client requirements for the work are complete, they are copied to the work-in-progress requirements register (5). The performance and resource requirements for the work are established and entered into the work packages register (6).

As the work progresses, the work management team:

- Deals with issues with the requirements at the bottom of figure 5.

- Reports performance data in the work packages register (6).

- Captures, resolves, and reports on softer issues through the events register (2).

The model is:

- The backbone of the communications strategy.

- The complete flexible and robust fence between a client organization in blue and the solution provider organization in green.

- A complete and shareable work plan.

All team members have read privileges to a targeted, information-rich, and living work plan. When things change, as they always do, team members will know what has changed and why. They adjust their work accordingly.

Each of these registers has a history capability. If something goes awry with the work, a check over this work communications information model is revealing. Identify the issue and correct it. The team moves on, maintaining focus on the work and not pointing fingers!

I could browse and see the state of the work at any moment, avoiding unnecessary interventions.

Communications: Key Points

- Too much information is as bad as too little when it comes to team performance.

- The better the understanding of the work, the better the supporting information model.

- Information is more accurate when used frequently. Use the information model for your work.

- Make communications part of the work process and not a stand-alone activity.

- Integrate team communications in the information model supporting the work.

- The better the information model:

  · The less time is spent in resource wasting activities.

  · The more team members are able to appropriately adjust their work.

- Information can be volatile—a note might have a short life) —or durable—a policy document. Handle them accordingly.

BOTTOM LINE: Access to relevant information is critical in the pursuit of results.

Notes

Chapter 11
CONCLUSION

In the early 1980s, authors Peters and Waterman went in search of excellence, and they found it in many places. Looking back on my work experiences, I would have to say that excellence can be found wherever one finds a collection of people who communicate well together, are suited to the work, and are appropriately led and managed. The probability that excellence will be found increases if that group of people have the right attitude, the right approach to their work, and the ability to apply themselves to the task.

The ten objectives in this book describe an approach to teamwork that has been successful on more than one occasion and under several different conditions. The common threads through these objectives are:

- A focus on the work.

- A style of communication that is integral to every activity or task.

- People who generally identify with the qualities described in chapters 1 and 2.

In describing the approach, a picture of the required attitude develops, as does a functional information model that supports the human discipline necessary for sustained activity. In the picture of the right attitude, "thinking" stands at the front and centre of the image.

Thinking, along with the managed flexibility to act, builds

self-confidence and self-esteem. People just feel better about themselves. Such a thing cannot be mandated, it is encouraged. This book has talked about how to be successful at that in the work environment by developing a level of interest and focus on the work. It is an evolutionary process.

The right work environment requires no special tools. Everything that is needed is right there in the workplace. Like language is a combination of what is said and how it is said, so the workplace is about what and how things are done. Just as you can change the meaning of the same words through delivery, you can change the workplace by how you use its constituent parts.

Success in the challenge is not an individual effort. It requires the right attitude, approach, and application across the team. This book has talked about supporting and encouraging those qualities in a team and increasing the sustainable performance level independent of the mechanics that define its purpose. It could be an accounting team, a project management team, and so on

There are numerous books and courses available on management and leadership subjects such as enterprise architecture, requirements engineering, systems engineering, project or program management, finance, accounting, and outward-bound adventure training, to name a few. Such books, much like *In Search of Excellence*, raise the awareness of the content of the subject matter. It is practice that develops skill in the application of this knowledge and this experience builds the professional vocabulary and pattern recognition referred to in chapter 2.

When armed with the knowledge these courses provide, it is important to think about how this knowledge can be best applied in your particular situation. There are countless good ideas that can be applied to a logically stupid conclusion and when that happens, failure nearly always results. These failures are less likely to happen when a team is thinking and communication is integrated with the work. Why? The situational awareness that thinking and effective team communication develops, enables discussions that help avoid failures. Failures can still occur, but they should be less numerous and tend to be less significant.

The same applies to the content of this book. You do not have to be good everywhere at everything. I have never done everything in this book all at once, although I have done it all at least once, I think!

Of the eight teams I have managed and led, one was independently assessed as excellent, one other would have met that assessment had that occurred, and the other six all put in decent performances, meeting the objectives set by my bosses within their timeline and budget constraints. Had those teams had to rise to the challenge of excellence, there is no doubt in my mind many of them would have cleared that performance bar! Excellence does not happen overnight; it takes preparation with the team and then the opportunity to excel. I don't believe people can be excellent all the time.

I accepted the people in place and when people moved on, I chose the best person for the work. I avoided people who would tell me what I wanted to hear. The best person for the job would give me their point of view. My point here? Good team performance is not dependent on a particular demographic or all friends together. People, regardless of their demographic, who possess the right attitude and ability to apply themselves to the task at hand, can, with the right approach to their work, achieve excellence or at least perform well when in the right group. As a manager/leader, it is your non-delegable job to build that group!

I recall one team was a particularly eclectic mix. I think every team member had a particular distinguishing demographic identifier. There is a collection of different sensitivities that have to be considered and taken into account when getting the best from your team. It is a leadership challenge to find the right balance, and it is super critical to be seen as fair and even handed. Regardless of what has been written in this book, if you as a manager/leader are not seen to be fair and even handed, the team will not perform at its best. When the group is built and you find yourself with an eclectic mix, do not avoid the challenge—run to it, embrace it, and learn from it.

Teams That Pop talks about evolving teams and developing people. As a supervising manager, this includes you. From this book, you should comprehend that a supervising manager needs to be prepared to adjust their style to meet the needs of the team. For the managers and leaders amongst us, if you want more out of your team, perhaps consider if your management and leadership style is too far away from how your team wants to be managed or led. Can you bring it closer?

This book can be a handy reference to glance at if something is not working right to see if the cause might jump out at you. The key points of each chapter are listed in part three, "Retrospective on the Book," for your easy reference should you need it.

Conclusion: Key Points

– Focus on the work.

– Communication is integral to the work, not a separate function.

– The work environment encourages the right behaviours, thinking, and the managed flexibility to act. Thus, people build self-confidence, self-esteem, and generally feel better about themselves. They will be more productive.

– Nothing special is required for the right work environment. All the elements are right there. It is how they are used that is important.

– Courses provide the knowledge; practice develops the skills.

– There is no place for racism, sexism, agism, or any of the isms on a good team. Choose the best person available for the job every time!

BOTTOM LINE: Excellence can be found wherever one finds a collection of people who communicate well together, are suited to the work, and are appropriately led and managed.

PART THREE:

RETROSPECTIVE ON THE BOOK

I:
ROUTE TO THE BOOK

While the story proper starts in the mid- to late 1990s, there were two events in the 1980s that are relevant to the story. The first was picking up Peters and Waterman's *In Search of Excellence* in the early 1980s. There are many good management practices described in this book. I added many of them to my toolbox for use in my first proper management and leadership jobs, where I enjoyed some early success.

The second was from 1985 to 1987, when I served in *Her Majesty's Canadian Ship Nipigon* as the marine systems engineering officer. We did very well at the mid-cycle workups. The team popped! While we did implement a very active training program over the two years prior, the team's performance was more than a training program could reasonably explain. I did not have the experience to know what that was.

It was 1997 before the topic came up again. I was on a course at The Institute, which was a Canadian federal government training facility managed and operated by Public Works and Government Services Canada. The subject of the course was "Managing the IT/IM Function," and it was delivered by Dr. Walter Baker. If my memory is correct, this is when I first heard the idea that "A manager's role is to release the power of their team." On hearing this, my immediate thought was, "This is self-evident." It was exactly what had happened during that workups period, ten years prior. But it still did not illuminate the details for me!

My understanding from that course was that managers had to adjust their style to suit the team, to get the most out of the collection of individuals. A manager that was too controlling restricted the team to their power, while a manager that was too laissez-faire for their team lost efficiency and effectiveness. It was from here that I started to adjust my management style toward the team and adopted my understanding of Dr. Baker's thinking on objectives and results management, which I started to practice on return to the workplace. For the purposes of this book, team one.

At that time (1995 to 2002), I was employed at the National Defence Headquarters, Ottawa, supporting the procurement and maintenance of ships and ship systems. My director general at that time, Commodore Wayne Gibson, created an uncomplicated work management system to optimize the wise expenditure of his budget. It worked very well. I was fortunate enough to be the staff officer who oversaw the daily activities in building and putting this information system to work. From a ring side seat, I observed several lessons, which were applied to my future work.

- For a work management system to work and be accurate, it must be accessible to the team and used for its purpose.

- To be used for its purpose, the information in the system must fill an obvious need. The supervising manager was clear and precise about the information needed to do the work and why it was needed.

- The importance of the question: What's the work?

In the early 2000s, I moved on to my next team, which was tasked to develop an enterprise architecture framework based on systems engineering principles. The team developed a set of information artifacts for each level in what is called a system baseline. There were six baseline levels in our model: concept, functional, architectural, design, product, and operational. The model facilitated communications between the various stakeholders. It worked very well, advancing several projects that had hitherto become bogged down in process.

During this period, I had the pleasure of attending a course on the Zachman Framework delivered by John Zachman. If my memory is correct, he articulated the following thought: "The framework should help you think about things." This was something I found to be true of enterprise architecture as a subject. It should help you think about how an organization operates.

In the later part of this decade, I moved to team three, where the task was to provide a full-service support (technology system and subject expertise) in requirements engineering. It was in this team that, with the help of one of the younger team members, Mr. Kevin Jackson, I developed my understanding of the then Telelogic now IBM tool, Dynamic Object-Oriented Requirements Software (DOORS). For two to three years, my focus was completely on requirements management and at the end of that period, I concluded that it was more helpful to a successful implementation to consider requirements as representing the understanding—as distinct from a hard and fast statement of requirement—of the need at the time the requirements were written. This understanding frequently evolves as the work progresses and time passes. Better to be prepared for discussion and evolution as distinct to defending something for reasons that are not helpful to the end goal.

During this period, I attended a user conference in Austin, Texas, on IBM Rational software products. During one of the enterprise architecture sessions, the presenter (I cannot recall his name, unfortunately) pointed out the error many people make with defining, explaining, or otherwise considering processes: they often include decision logic. This was another idea that once heard was, to me, self-evident. Going forward from there, I adopted the practice to keep process diagrams clear of decision logic and confine such relevant content to procedural type documents.

At the end of this period, support was withdrawn for the requirements management initiative and many other teams were transferred in under my oversight. Team four.

My work evolved toward client relationship and team management across multiple aspects of the larger organization: policing, technical document (drawings and publications) management, customs, supply and inventory, and so on. I used my newly acquired expertise in DOORS to oversee the requirements for each of these areas, the work that the teams were doing toward results for the clients, and the resource management for this work. For budget management, with some simple code, it was possible to make a DOORS module work like a spreadsheet. I found this particularly useful to track year-on-year performance. I had created an information environment that met the overall requirements of the work management system I referred to in the period from 1995 to 2002, with one big advantage. The environment could be easily adjusted and amended to meet changes in the overall and detailed evolving requirements without the need of an IT tech to make the changes. As a manager, I had empowered myself.

The next challenge appeared in 2011: teams five and six. In-service-support contracts are normally associated with physical equipment that can be delivered into an external contractor's hands for maintenance and repair. There is a separation between the operational and maintenance environments. The idea of an in-service-support contract for an information system is something different because the separation is not present. To achieve the benefit of an in-service-support contract, the external contractor must work independently—to the greatest extent possible—in the body of the main network. Access to and operations in the interior of complex government networks is tightly managed—as one might expect. The challenge was to oversee the contractors' work in a way that allows their freedom to work as a private sector company in a tightly regulated government environment.

Progress in our approach to the problem was accelerated by a high priority project originating high up in government. Team five delivered the project well inside time and budget expectations. Evidence in the user community indicated the delivered product was well used in the first year of operations. The information model (figure 5) was a product of our success in this project. This team popped!

The answer to the question I posed to myself in 1987— How did that happen?—was there in front of me. The right combination of leadership, management, and followership skills distributed in the team, supported by the right approach to the work and access to accurate information required to guide and progress the work, will motivate people with the ability to apply themselves, to get the job done and done right!

Team six implemented the information model (figure 5) in the steady state operation.

II:
SUMMARY LIST OF KEY POINTS

Introduction: Key Points

- The objective of this book is to provide managers with an approach to solving the problem of team performance that is within their reach.

- A significant direct investment should not be required.

- The emphasis is on enriching the work environment.

- The book is not about a specific team or industry. It is written to apply to many teams.

- There are several big wins that are attractive to investors, managers, and employees alike.

- The solution features leadership qualities to develop and maintain a suitable work culture and management skills to guide the team toward its goals.

BOTTOM LINE: Good management makes good managers makes teams that pop!

The Problem: Key Points

- People are the source of energy in the workplace.

- The more energy the team members bring to the work-place, the more work gets done.

- We want to make it easier for people to work at their capacity for work, and then use that capacity wisely.

BOTTOM LINE: The problem is how to maximize the amount of energy a team can apply to the work by making better use of what is available rather than acquiring something new.

The Approach: Key Points

- How to nurture a successful work culture is what we need to understand.

- Focus on three things:

  · Team interactions.

  · Understanding the work.

  · Encouraging personal development.

- Frame the approach through goal, vision, and mission statements. Mark the route to success with objectives and a results plan.

BOTTOM LINE: The right ATTITUDE brings with it an openness to find the right APPROACH and the individual APPLICATION to see the task through to completion.

The Solution: Key Points

– The management model is a three-layer cake comprised of twelve components.

– For any team, the parts to this cake will have a different preparation, mix, and integration to achieve a well-performing team that is resilient in change.

– A person's compatibility with their work and work culture is a factor in the amount of energy released for work.

– Choosing the right people for the work is critical to good team performance.

– Develop the model through the parallel pursuit of ten objectives.

BOTTOM LINE: The model evolves through a complex, almost organic process. The components generally develop in parallel and at a different pace, not sequentially.

Implementation: Key Points

– There are four steps: pick the leader, start the culture, develop the model, and continuously improve.

– Results objectives should be challenging but not exhausting.

– To ensure the team remains at its best, continue to seek improvements through small changes that can be reversed if required.

BOTTOM LINE: A culture appropriate to the workplace that is guided by an effective, efficient, and economic management model will, in a continuous improvement activity, generate the right environment and get results.

The Supervising Manager: Key Points

- Supervising managers provide the core for the culture.

- During the process they:

  - Oversee the evolution of the team.

  - Encourage thinking and initiative.

  - Keep the "good-idea fairies" in check.

  - Ensure the team does not wander off course and lose sight of its goal.

  - Identify and use situations to address weaknesses.

  - Integrate weakness and strength to generate a whole.

  - Are fair and even handed.

  - Recruit the best available people for the work.

- Supervising managers keep their heads up to look over, around, and into the team to keep it safe and on track.

- Relationship building and supporting attitudes are columns around which the team can form.

- Releasing the power of the team is about building on something that is stable and functioning.

- Resist the temptation to make your mark.

- Understand the work before beginning the transformation.

- Encourage the expression of honestly held views.

- Resolve issues or accept them as facts of life that one must work with.

BOTTOM LINE: The supervising manager sets the tone for the team from day one. They provide the leadership for the evolving culture and supervision for the developing management model.

Establishing the Culture: Key Points

- People are the source of team energy. Culture determines how much of that energy is released for work.

- A better management model encourages people to give their energy, is open to receiving it, and is better at using it.

- Commitment to certain behaviour patterns is a make or break item.

- Management, leadership, and followership are not separate entities. They are commodities distributed throughout the team.

- There are several positive core behaviours: openness, straightforwardness, understanding, flexibility, relationship building, respectfulness, and competence.

- There are several positive enhancing factors: decision-making/taking ability, communication skills, knowledge, experience, attitude, and intelligence.

- Supervising managers set the behaviour example and assign and monitor individual development work.

- Team members actively support the list of behaviours.

- Team members are curious about their work. They are active in the development of the management infrastructure. Question it and work to improve it.

- The target culture cannot be forced. Team chemistry must form naturally and that requires time and patience.

- Relationships in the team are fundamental to success.

- Team members should come to work:

  · To get things done.

  · Be prepared to engage.

  · Be prepared to take direction or lead as required.

- Management and leadership are not popularity contests. It is about getting the job done and doing it right, on time, and under budget.

- Management structures should not be too tightly integrated or overly prescriptive.

- A thinking-empowered team that is aware of its environment and accepts individual responsibility is essential to generating and sustaining the target culture.

BOTTOM LINE: Developing management, leadership, and followership abilities throughout the team generates a robust team that will get results.

Policies, Processes, Procedures, and Practices: Key Points

- The 4 P's:

  - Are essential. Keep them to the minimum.

  - Guide the work and should not get in its way.

  - Are the heart of the management model.

- If people understand the benefit of what they are being asked to do, they generally will do it better.

- Understanding the work will lead to leaner, more tightly focussed guiding documents.

- Discussing these documents will generate a better understanding.

- Teams need to take ownership.

- Avoid embedding decision logic in process.

- Keep integration as loose as possible to retain flexibility.

BOTTOM LINE: Team participation in the development of the 4 P's improves the understanding of the work, which leads to a better end product in this area.

The Work: Key Points

- The culture and the management model develop around the work.

- Understand the work. Like a ball, look at it from all angles.

- Encourage team discussion and do more listening.

- Suggest solutions to problem areas and accept feedback.

- Leaving things to sit for a while is seldom a bad idea.

- Make sure everyone has something that interests them and something not so interesting on their plate.

- Keeping work interesting keeps people interested in working.

BOTTOM LINE: Priorities (the what and why), resources (the who), and the efficacy of the 4 P's (the when, where, why, and how) constrain the work. The better the team understands the answers to these questions, the better their performance will be.

Role-Based Team Structures: Key Points

- Create a role-based organizational structure which allows people a certain level of freedom—in their role—to do their work.

- Ensure team members understand the team roles and their role in the team.

- If possible, switch the team members in their roles to freshen things up from time to time.

BOTTOM LINE: Role-based teams support a broader knowledge of the work. As a result, the team is more resilient in change.

Work Planning: Key Points

- Work plans are critical to the communications required to support the development of the culture.

- Work plans guide the available energy to the work.

- Effective work planning maximizes the value of the work.

- Effective work plans have a planning horizon that suit the environment in which they are used.

- The nature of an organization's priorities and how they change is a factor in the mix when determining a planning horizon.

- Priority management is a crucial component of work planning.

- Effective priority management is critical to maximizing the value of the work and supporting stable work plans.

BOTTOM LINE: Effective planning of the work is the foundation for results and an enabler for the culture.

Results: Key Points

- Results don't just happen, they are targeted and achieved.

- A work planning cycle will contain many results planning cycles.

- Interaction between the supervising manager and the team is a must.

- There are several tactics available which can work

separately or together. They must be consistent and aligned, not divergent.

- Work review meetings.
- Events register.
- Team meetings.
- Maintaining an open-door policy.
- Management by walking around.
- Performance reviews; meetings with individuals.

BOTTOM LINE: Results are achieved by setting reasonable targets and maintaining focus in all team interactions.

Requirements Management: Key Points

- Requirements describe something you want or need.

- The level of detail and assessment of a requirement are influenced by the relationship between a client and their solution provider.

- In the "good fences makes good neighbours" proverb, requirements are the fence between a client and their solution provider.

- Requirements work stops when the work is complete and not before.

- Changes to requirements do happen. Plan to adjust or change written requirements during the process, or plan to fail.

- Effective requirement change management influences the relationship between client and solution provider.

- Should things start to go wrong in the work, a focus on requirements can defuse situations.

BOTTOM LINE: Requirements show an understanding of the work and support the communication of that understanding between those wanting the work completed (the client) and those doing the work (the solution provider).

Change Management: Key Points

- To build a healthy team it is especially important to encourage ideas, suggestions, and dialogue and act upon them.

- A change starts with the idea that something is wrong or could be better.

- To describe the change, answer the following questions:

  · What is the background?

  · What is the deficiency?

  · What is the objective?

  · What are the highest-level requirements?

  · What do you expect the solution to look like?

- An incremental and gated approach allows risk-managed progress with a formal off-ramp at the end of each stage.

- Initiation. How big is the task? What should the budget and timeframe be? What are the options and risks involved?

- Discovery. Develop the options to indicative estimates of cost and schedule. Confirm the answers to the questions in the initiation section.

- Assessment. Develop the preferred option(s) to substantive estimates of cost and schedule. Confirm the answers to the questions in the initiation section. Describe what the product or service must do and how it will be assessed.

- Development. Build the product or service.

- Implementation. This is industry specific.

- Closure. Evaluate any gap in expectations and what to do about it. Separate records required for future use from those that will not be required.

– The first three stages (initiate, discovery, and assessment) are the "thinking about it" phase.

– The last three stages (development, implementation, and in-service) are the "doing it" phase, where the change is actively and vigorously prosecuted.

– Effective requirements management supports a satisfactory outcome for both the client and the solution provider.

BOTTOM LINE: Change management is a non-discretionary and critical piece of the management framework.

Communications: Key Points

– Too much information is as bad as too little when it comes to team performance.

– The better the understanding of the work, the better the supporting information model.

– Information is more accurate when used frequently. Use the information model for your work.

– Make communications part of the work process and not a stand-alone activity.

– Integrate team communications in the information model supporting the work.

– The better the information model:

  · The less time is spent on resource-wasting activities.

  · The more team members are able to appropriately adjust their work.

– Information can be volatile—a note might have a short life—or durable—a policy document. Handle them accordingly.

BOTTOM LINE: Access to relevant information is critical in the pursuit of results.

Conclusion: Key Points

– Focus on the work.

– Communications is integral to the work, not a separate function.

– The work environment encourages the right behaviours,
thinking, and the managed flexibility to act. Thus, people
build self-confidence, self-esteem, and generally feel better
about themselves. They will be more productive.

– Nothing special is required for the right work environment. All the elements are right there. It is how they are
used that is important.

– Courses provide the knowledge; practice develops
the skills.

– There is no place for racism, sexism, agism or any of the
-isms on a good team. Choose the best person available for
the job every time!

**BOTTOM LINE: Excellence can be found wherever one finds
a collection of people, who communicate well together, are
suited to the work, and are appropriately led and managed.**

III:
ACKNOWLEDGEMENTS

The content of this book is 100 percent based on my experience through forty plus years in the workforce. That experience did not happen in isolation, and section I part three of the book generally describes the path of that experience. Thinking about it now, that path started well before 1982. To recall and mention all the people who I have had the pleasure to work with over the years is, for me, an impossible task. Thank you all for all the interactions that led to this work!

When it came to the actual writing of this book, I needed a support team that would provide a variety of perspectives when they read and critiqued the presentation of the content. I was fortunate to have such people amongst my family, friends, and work-related relationships.

These people did a great and detailed job for me in the review of many versions of the manuscript. I thank them for their time, commitment, constructive criticism, and overall contribution to the work. Specifically, their varied perspectives facilitated the resolution of several issues that I struggled with regarding content and presentation. In alphabetical order, many thanks to Mary-Anne Carignan, Emeritus Professor Peter Lawrence, Laurie Carey (a big shout out here for her work on the cover design and title), Peter Martin, Christopher Nolan, Lynne Nolan (who was Lynne Blake during her management career), and Sean Tagieff. A big thank you to Shayne Morrissey for his work on the cover photo.

It would be remiss of me not to mention FRIESENPRESS here. Their processes and the people who supported them, were without exception first rate. Their value added to the end product is acknowledged here.

Lastly, there's a huge thank you to my family—Susan, Geoff, Chris, and Simon—for their love and support through a large part of my forty years in the workforce; especially Susan, for her patience, understanding, and contributions during the entire life experience and book writing process.